Everyman's Poetry

*Everyman, I will go with thee,
and be thy guide*

John Skelton

Selected and edited by GREG WALKER

University of Leicester

EVERYMAN
J. M. Dent · London

This edition first published by Everyman Paperbacks in 1997
Selection, introduction and other critical apparatus
© J. M. Dent 1997

J. M. Dent
Orion Publishing Group
Orion House
5 Upper St Martin's Lane,
London WC2H 9EA

Typeset by Deltatype Ltd, Birkenhead, Merseyside
Printed in Great Britain by
The Guernsey Press Co. Ltd, Guernsey, C. I.

British Library Cataloguing-in-Publication
Data is available upon request.

ISBN 0 460 87796 8

Contents

Note on the Author and Editor

JOHN SKELTON was born *c.* 1460, possibly in the north of England. He was laureated by the universities of Oxford, Cambridge and Louvain. He joined the royal household of Henry VII in 1488, taking holy orders a decade later. He acted as tutor to the future Henry VIII until the death of Prince Arthur in 1502, when his royal charge became heir apparent and Skelton was pensioned off to the rectory in Diss, Norfolk. The poet quickly returned to Westminster, however, on the accession of the young King, and the remainder of his career was characterised by a continuing and not always successful search for patronage from his former pupil. He was to produce the powerful satirical poetry for which he is chiefly remembered during the last twenty years of his life, while he resided in a tenement in the Sanctuary of Westminster Abbey, writing with one eye always on the court and the other on the powerful merchant communities of the City of London who were his other major source of patronage. He died 21 June 1529 and was buried in St Margaret's Westminster.

GREG WALKER is Reader in Medieval and Early Renaissance English Literature at the University of Leicester. He has written a number of books and articles on Skelton's life and works, including *John Skelton and the Politics of the 1520s* (Cambridge, 1988), and material in *Plays of Persuasion: Drama and Politics at the Court of Henry VIII* (Cambridge, 1991) and *Persuasive Fictions* (Scolar Press, 1996).

Chronology of Skelton's Life and Times

1512   At request of Abbot Islip, Skelton produces epitaph for
        Henry VII to adorn his tomb in Westminster Abbey

1513   Henry VIII invades France, and wins victories at
        Thérouanne and Battle of the Spurs; meanwhile English
        forces under Thomas Howard, Earl of Surrey, defeat the
        Scots at Flodden. Skelton writes propaganda pieces in
        support of the war effort, including *A Ballad of the
        Scottish King* (printed by Fakes almost immediately upon
        completion) and *Against the Scots*. Skelton begins to style
        himself 'Orator Regius' in works written at this time

1514   Writes the series of flytyng poems *Against Garnesche* at
        suggestion of Henry VIII. Thomas Wolsey becomes
        Archbishop of York

1515   Writes epitaph for Lady Margaret Beaufort, mother of
        Henry VII, for display in Westminster Abbey. Wolsey
        becomes a cardinal and Lord Chancellor of England

1516–17 Writes *The Tunning of Elynour Rummyng*

1519   Sides with traditionalist Robert Whittinton and the
        'Trojans' in their struggle against the Humanist 'Greeks'
        in the so-called Grammarians' War among scholars. A
        number of Henry VIII's closest companions are briefly
        expelled from court – an event probably reflected in
        Skelton's only surviving dramatic work, *Magnificence*,
        written at this time

1520   Henry VIII meets Francis I at Field of Cloth of Gold

1521   Cardinal Wolsey chairs Calais peace conference between
        France and the Empire. Skelton writes first of his satires
        against Wolsey, *Speak, Parrot*. Autumn: Skelton produces
        second of his anti-Wolsey poems, *Colin Cloute*

1522   Third anti-Wolsey satire, *Why Come Ye Not to Court?*,
        completed

1523   Makes peace with Wolsey, who commissions him to write
        a poem attacking the Scottish Regent, the Duke of
        Albany. Skelton fulsomely dedicates completed work,
        How the Douty Duke of Albany . . . , to Wolsey. Perhaps as
        a result of the poet's new-found favour, an earlier poem,
        The Garland of Laurel, much reworked, is published by
        Fakes on 3 October

1525   First edition of William Tyndale's English translation of the
        New Testament printed in Cologne

1527   Henry VIII expresses doubts about the validity of his
        marriage to Katherine of Aragon, which lead in time to
        the break with Rome and Henry's marriage to Anne
        Boleyn
1528   Skelton, whose interests turned to the defence of religious
        orthodoxy in his last years, attends judicial abjuration of
        convicted heretic, Thomas Bowgas, and writes last
        surviving work, the *Replication*, against two other
        convicted heretics, Thomas Bilney and Thomas Arthur
1529   Dies 21 June and is buried in St Margaret's Westminster,
        before the high altar

Introduction

John Skelton is perhaps the greatest 'unknown' poet of English literature. A true idiosyncratic genius, he has a tendency to fall between accepted categories and classifications and become lost to sight. Too scurrilous to be a part of the Great Poetic Tradition of Wyatt, Surrey and Spenser, yet too evidently learned and brilliant to be dismissed as a mere wordsmith, he presents difficulties for anthologisers and the devisers of university syllabuses alike. Too late for the last great flowering of late medieval poetry, and too early for the first pre-natal flutterings of the Renaissance, Skelton is generally seen, if he is seen at all, as a transitional figure, interesting more for what he points towards than what he offers in his own terms. Yet he is in himself almost a complete history of the verse of his period, moving from the typically 'medieval', heavily conventional, aureate style of his first memorial poems and love lyrics to the distinctively eccentric mode of his later satires and longer poems, characteristically written in the 'Skeltonic' verse form which he made his own. Here the leashes of short lines, rhyming on a single sound for often upwards of a dozen lines, created a poetic voice which was much copied in subsequent decades, but no one was to master the form with anything like Skelton's assurance or splenetic energy. In this great harnessing of the vibrancy and affective potential of the English language, often intermingled with snatches of French and Latin in true macaronic style, the poet suggests the forces which were to characterise the distinctively ambitious and iconoclastic verse of the English Renaissance.

Although it is thus tempting to see the poet as representative of wider movements and themes, however, the most powerful resonances in his work are much more immediate and specific. Skelton's poetry is almost always occasional in the sense that it is prompted by a particular event, moment, place, or person. It is the white heat of personal animosity that prompts the vitriolic invective of his poems against the anonymous 'Comely Coystowne' (dismissed as 'This doctor devious, commenced in a cart / A master[?] A minstrel, a fiddler, a fart[!]') or against 'Old John Clarke', the unfortunate parishioner of Diss, whose death prompted the poet to memorialise him in a scurrilous Trental:

Bibite multum:
Ecce sepultum
Sub pede stultum
Asinum et mulum!
The devill kis[s] his *culum!*

[Drink deep: / Behold buried / Under foot a foolish / Ass and mule /
The Devil kiss his arse]

And indeed Skelton's is a particularly vitriolic muse. Whereas
the majority of Tudor poets felt it expedient to turn their hands to
the poetry of patronage and supplication, shaping their verses 'to'
and 'on' people and places, Skelton's characteristic mode was to
write 'against' individuals, whether they were lowly East Anglian
townsfolk or the chief minister of the realm. Thus the poet found
himself frequently involved in the controversies of his time. When a
dispute blew up between scholars over the correct manner of
teaching Latin and Greek, the poet sided with the traditionalists,
dubbed the 'Trojans' by their humanistic opponents owing to their
hostility to the modish teaching of Greek. In the heat of the dispute
the poet wrote against the reformers and was in turn memorably
abused by the Humanist William Lily:

Skelton thou art, let all men know it
Neither learned, nor a poet.

The poet's most memorable courting of controversy came in
1521, with the writing of the first of his three satires against
Thomas Wolsey. Wolsey at that time was at the height of his
powers as Lord Chancellor of the realm, cardinal and papal legate,
and Henry VIII's chief confidant and minister. Skelton clearly
thought that he could detect the first signs of a rift between king and
cardinal, however, growing out of the latter's lengthy sojourn in
Calais, where he was convening a peace conference between
France and the Empire. Skelton turned criticisms of Wolsey's
conduct into the substance of his satirical poem, *Speak, Parrot*,
hoping thereby to catch the mood of the moment and attract royal
favour. The resulting poem, a fantastic conceit, comparable to
Eliot's *Waste Land* in its capacity to evoke a vision of a society and a
culture in crisis, was, however, too cryptic for its first courtly
readers. Thus the poet was forced to add increasingly specific and
shrill supplementary *Envoys* to it, pointing out the centrality of the

Calais Conference and Wolsey's personality to his vision of the ills of the world. Finally, he abandoned the project and adopted a more direct satirical form instead, continuing the assault on Wolsey in two further satires, *Colin Cloute* and *Why Come Ye Not to Court?* In the former, the poet adopts the persona of Colin, an honest rustic figure familiar to readers of classical pastoral verse, who laments the divisions between clergy and laity which he claims to see all around him. In the venerable medieval tradition of anti-clerical satire, Skelton turns Colin's lament into an attack upon the alleged vices and corruption of the contemporary clergy, but keeps the reader's gaze firmly upon Wolsey, who is painted as both the embodiment and the inspiration of the fallen state of the Church. In *Why Come Ye Not to Court?*, Skelton speaks in the voice of an ageing counsellor, driven from court by the excesses of Wolsey's administration, and now free to point out the follies of a realm in which, he claims, the cardinal usurps the place of the king, and sets up his own court at Hampton Court, from which he leads the realm to ruin.

The passion and vitriol of these later satires has led many readers to assume that Skelton's hatred of Wolsey was real and intense, and that the picture of Henrician England which he paints is realistic. The truth seems to have been rather different, however. For as soon as Skelton saw that Wolsey was not about to fall from favour, and that his poetic assaults were not finding favour with his intended royal audience, he abandoned the project and began to write for, rather than against Wolsey. His next poems were indeed dedicated to the cardinal in fulsome terms. Having found that he could not win patronage by beating Wolsey, Skelton seems to have decided to join him instead, and turned his satiric pen against the enemies of the realm and the evangelical reformers who threatened the Church.

As the quotation from Juvenal with which he concludes *Why Come Ye Not To Court?* suggests, Skelton found it difficult *not* to write satire. The poems collected in this volume are all in some way touched by the spirit of irony or invective. Even the early love lyrics, with which this selection begins, have a raucous and often bitterly misogynist sexual agenda, while *Philip Sparrow*, in many ways the poet's most charming creation, falls eventually into a voyeuristic and not uncritical 'appreciation' of its young recipient's physical attributes. In this as in all his work Skelton brings his own unmistakable voice to the conventional material he rehearses.

GREG WALKER

John Skelton

Womanhood, Wanton, Ye Want

Womanhood, wanton, ye want;
   Your meddling, mistress, is mannerless;
Plenty of ill, of goodness scant,
   Ye rail at riot, recheles:
   To praise your porte it is needless;
For all your draffe yet and your dregs,
As well borne as ye full oft time begs.

Why so coy and full of scorn?
   Mine horse is sold, I wene, you say;
My new furred gown, when it is worn,   10
   Put up your purse, ye shall not pay.
   By creed, I trust to see the day,
As proud a pohen as ye spread,
Of me and other ye may have need.

Though angelic be your smiling,
   Yet is your tongue an adder's tail,
Full like a scorpion stinging
   All those by whom ye have avail:
   Good mistress Anne, there ye do shail:
What prate ye, pretty piggesny?   20
I trust to quit you ere I die.

Your key is meet for every lock,
   Your key is common and hangeth out;
Your key is ready, we need not knock,
   Nor stand long wresting there about;
   Of your door-gate ye have no doubt:
But one thing is, that ye be lewd:
Hold your tongue now, all beshrewd!

To mistress Anne, that farly sweet,
That wones at the Key in Thames Street.   30

Lullay, Lullay, Like a Child

With, Lullay, lullay, like a child,
Thou sleepest too long, thou art beguiled.

My darling dear, my daisy flower,
    Let me, quod he, lie in your lap.
Lie still, quod she, my paramour,
    Lie still hardly, and take a nap.
    His head was heavy, such was his hap,
All drowsy dreaming, drowned in sleep,
That of his love he took no keep,
                    With, Hey, lullay, etc.

With ba, ba, ba, and bas, bas, bas,
    She cherished him both cheek and chin,
That he wist never where he was;   10
    He had forgotten all deadly sin.
    He wanted with her love to win:
He trusted her payment, and lost all his prey:
She left him sleeping, and stole away,
                    With, Hey, lullay, etc.

The rivers rowth, the waters wan;
    She spared not to wet her feet;
She waded over, she found a man
    That halsed her heartily and kissed her sweet:
    Thus after her cold she caught a heat.
My love, she said, rowteth in his bed;   20
I wis he hath an heavy head;
                    With, Hey, lullay, etc.

What dreamest thou, drunkard, drowsy pate!
    Thy lust and liking is from thee gone;
Thou blinkered blowboll, thou wakest too late,
    Behold, thou liest, luggard, alone!
    Well may thou sigh, well may thou groan,
To deal with her so cowardly:
I wis, pole hatchet, she bleared thine eye.

The Ancient Acquaintance

The ancient acquaintance, madam, between us twain,
    The familiarity, the former dalliance,
Causeth me that I can not myself refrain
    But that I must write for my pleasant pastaunce:
    Remembering your passing goodly countenance,
Your goodly port, your beauteous visage,
Ye may be counted comfort of all courage.

Of all your features favorable to make true description,
    I am insufficient to make such enterprise;
For thus dare I say, without contradiction,   10
    That Dame Menolope was never half so wise:
        Yet so it is that a rumour beginneth for to rise,
How in good horsemen ye set your whole delight,
And have forgotten your old true loving knight,

With bound and rebound, bouncingly take up
    His gentle curtoil and set nought by small nags!
Spur up at the hinder girth, with, Gup, morell, gup!
    With, Jayst ye, jenet of Spain, for your tail wags!
    Ye cast all your courage upon such courtly hags.
Have in sergeant ferrour, mine horse behind is bare;   20
He rideth well the horse, but he rideth better the mare.

Ware, ware, the mare winceth with her wanton heel!
    She kicketh with her kalkins and killeth with a clench;
She goeth wide behind, and heweth never a deal:
    Ware galling in the withers, ware of the wrench!
    It is perilous for a horseman to dig in the trench.
This grieveth your husband, that right gentle knight,
And so with your servants he fiercely doth fight.

So fiercely he fighteth, his mind is so fell,
That he driveth them down with dints on their day watch   30
He bruiseth their brainpans and maketh them to swell,
    Their brows all to-broken, such claps they catch;
    Whose jealousy malicious maketh them to leap the hatch;

By their cognisance knowing how they serve a wily pie:
Ask all your neighbours whether that I lie.

It can be no counsel that is cried at the Cross:
　For your gentle husband sorrowful am I;
How be it, he is not first hath had a loss:
　Advertising you, madame, to work more secretly,
　Let not all the world make an outcry;　　　　　　　　40
Play fair play, madame, and look ye play clean,
Or else with great shame your game will be seen.

Ware the Lizard

Though ye suppose all jeopardies are past,
　And all is done that ye looked for before,
Ware yet, I rede you, of Fortune's double cast,
　For one false point she is wont to keep in store,
　And under the fell oft festered is the sore:
That when ye think all danger for to pass,
Ware of the lizard lieth lurking in the grass.

Mannerly Margery Milk and Ale

Aye, beshrew you, by my fay,
These wanton clerkes be nice always;
Avaunt, avaunt, my popagay!
What, will ye do nothing but play?
'Tully, valy', 'strawe', let be, I say!
Gup, Christian Cloute, gup, Jack of the Vale!
With, Mannerly Margery Milk and Ale.

By God, ye be a pretty pode,
And I love you an whole cart load.

Straw, James foder, ye play the fode,   10
I am no hackney for your road;
Go watch a bowl, your back is broad:
Gup, Christian Cloute, gup, Jack of the Vale!
With, Mannerly Margery Milk and Ale.

I wis ye deal uncourteously;
What would ye frumple me? now, fie!
What, and ye shall be my piggesny?
By Christ, ye shall not, no hardily;
I will not be japed bodily:
Gup, Christian Cloute, gup, Jack of the Vale!   20
With, Mannerly Margery Milk and Ale.

Walk forth your way, ye cost me nought;
Now have I found that I have sought,
The best cheap flesh that ever I bought.
Yet, for His love that all hath wrought,
Wed me, or else I die for thought!
Gup, Christian Cloute, your breath is stale!
Go, Mannerly Margery Milk and Ale!
Gup, Christian Cloute, gup, Jack of the Vale!
With, Mannerly Margery Milk and Ale.   30

To Mistress Margaret Hussey

Merry Margaret,
As Midsummer flower,
Gentle as falcon
Or hawk of the tower;

  With solace and gladness,
Much mirth and no madness,
All good and no badness,
So joyously,

So maidenly,
So womanly   10
Her demeaning
In every thing,
Far, far passing
That I can indict,
Or suffice to write
Of Merry Margaret,
As Midsummer flower,
Gentle as falcon
Or hawk of the tower;

        As patient and as still,   20
And as full of good will,
As fair Isaphill;
Colyaunder,
Sweet pommander,
Good Cassaunder;
Steadfast of thought,
Well made, well wrought;
Far may be sought
Erst that ye can find
So courteous, so kind   30
As merry Margaret,
This Midsummer flower,
Gentle as falcon
Or hawk of the tower.

To Mistress Gertrude Statham

Though ye were hard hearted,
And I with you thwarted
With words that smarted,
Yet now doubtless ye give me cause
To write of you this goodly clause,
Mistress Gertrude,
With womanhood endued,

With virtue well renewed.
   I will that ye shall be
In all benignity   10
Like to Dame Pasiphe;
For now doubtless ye give me cause
To write of you this goodly clause,
Mistress Gertrude,
With womanhood endued,
With virtue well renewed.
   Partly by your counsel,
Garnished with laurel
Was my fresh coronel;
Wherfore doubtless ye give me cause   20
To write of you this goodly clause,
Mistress Gertrude,
With womanhood endued,
With virtue well renewed.

Against a Comely Coystrowne

Against a comely coystrowne, that curiously chanted, and currishly
countered, and madly in his musics mockishly made against the
nine Muses of politic poems and poets matriculate.

Of all nations under the heaven,
   These frantic fools I hate most of all;
For though they stumble in the sins seven,
   In peevishness yet they snapper and fall,
   Which men the eighth deadly sin call.
This peevish proud, this prendergest,
When he is well, yet can he not rest.

A sweet sugar loaf and sour bayard's bun
   Be somedeal like in form and shape,
The one for a duke, the other for dun,   10
   A maunchet for morell thereon to snap.

His heart is too high to have any hap;
But for in his gamut carp that he can,
Lo, Jack would be a gentleman!

With, Hey, trolly, lolly, lo, whip here, Jack,
    Alumbek sodildem sillorim ben!
Curiously he can both counter and knack
    Of Martin Swart and all his merry men.
    Lord, how Perkin is proud of his pohen!
But ask where he findeth among his monachords   20
An holy water clerk a ruler of lords.

He cannot find it in rule nor in space:
    He solfeth too haught, his treble is too high;
He braggeth of his birth, that born was full base;
    His music without measure, too sharp is his 'my';
    He trimmeth in his tenor to counter pirdewy;
His descant is busy, it is without a mean;
Too fat is his fancy, his wit is too lean.

He lumbreth on a lewd lute, Roty bully joyse,
    Rumble down, tumble down, hey go, now, now!   30
He fumbleth in his fingering all ugly good noise,
    It seemeth the sobbing of an old sow:
    He would be made much of, and he wist how;
Well sped in spindles and turning of tavels;
A bungler, a brawler, a picker of quarrels.

Comely he clappeth a pair of clavichords;
    He whistleth so sweetly, he maketh me to sweat;
His descant is dashed full of discords;
    A red angry man, but easy to entreat:
    An usher of the hall fain would I get,   40
To point this proud page a place and a room,
For Jack would be a gentleman, that late was a groom.

Jack would jet, and yet Jill said nay;
    He counteth in his countenance to check with the best:
A malapert medler that prieth for his prey,
    In a dish dare he rush at the ripest;

Dreaming in dumps to wrangle and to wrest:
He findeth a proportion in his prick song,
To drink at a draught a large and a long.

Nay, jape not with him, he is no small fool, 50
    It is a solemn sire and a sullen;
For lords and ladies learn at his school;
    He teacheth them so wisely to solf and to faine,
    That neither they sing prick song nor plain:
This doctor Devious commenced in a cart,
A master, a minstrel, a fiddler, a fart.

What though ye can counter *Custodi nos?*
    As well it becometh you, a parish town clerk,
To sing *Sospitati dedit egros*:
    Yet bear ye not too bold, to brawl nor to bark 60
    At me, that meddled nothing with your work:
Correct first thyself; walk, and be nought!
Deem what thou list, thou knowest not my thought.

A proverb of old, 'say well or be still':
    Ye are too unhappy occasions to find
Upon me to clatter, or else to say ill.
    Now have I showed you part of your proud mind;
    Take this in worth, the best is behind.
Written at Croydon by Crowland in the Clay,
On Candelmas even, the Kalends of May. 70

Philip Sparrow

Pla ce bo,
Who is there, who?
Di le xi,
Dame Margery;
Fa, re, my, my,
Wherefore and why, why?
For the soul of Philip Sparrow,

That was late slain at Carrow,
Among the Nuns Black,
For that sweet soul's sake,   10
And for all sparrows' souls,
Set in our bead-rolls,
Pater noster qui,
With an *Ave Mari*,
And with the corner of a Creed,
The more shall be your mead.

   When I remember again
How my Philip was slain
Never half the pain
Was between you twain,   20
Pyramus and Thisbe,
As then befell to me:
I wept and I wailed,
The tears down hailed;
But nothing it availed
To call Philip again,
Whom Gib our cat hath slain.

   Gib, I say, our cat
Worried her on that
Which I loved best: 30
It cannot be expressed
My sorrowful heaviness
But all without redress;
For within that stound,
Half slumbering, in a sound
I fell down to the ground.

   Unneth I cast mine eyes
Toward the cloudy skies:
But when I did behold
My sparrow dead and cold,   40
No creature but that would
Have rued upon me,
To behold and see
What heaviness did me pang;
Wherewith my hands I wrang,
That my sinews cracked,
As though I had been racked,
So pained and so strained,

That no life well-nigh remained.
   I sighed and I sobbed, 50
For that I was robbed
Of my sparrow's life.
O maiden, widow and wife,
Of what estate ye be,
Of high or low degree,
Great sorrow then ye might see,
And learn to weep at me!
Such pains did me fret,
That mine heart did beat,
My visage pale and dead, 60
Wan, and blue as lead;
The pangs of hateful death
Well-nigh had stopped my breath.
   Heu, heu, me,
That I am woe for thee!
Ad Dominum, cum tribularer, clamavi.
Of God nothing else crave I
But Philip's soul to keep
From the marees deep
Of Acheronte's well, 70
That is a flood of Hell;
And from the great Pluto,
The prince of endless woe;
And from foul Alecto,
With visage black and blue;
And from Medusa, that mare,
That like a fiend doth stare;
And from Megera's adders,
From ruffling of Philip's feathers,
And from her fiery sparkling, 80
For burning of his wings;
And from the smokes sour
Of Proserpina's bower;
And from the dens dark,
Where Cerberus doth bark,
Whom Theseus did afray,
Whom Hercules did outray,
As famous poets say;

From that hell-hound,
That lieth in chains bound,   90
With ghastly heads three,
To Jupiter pray we
That Philip preserved may be!
Amen, say ye with me!
    Do mi nus,
Help now, sweet Jesus!
Levavi oculos meos in montes:
Would God I had Zenophontes,
Or Socrates the wise,
To show me their devise,   100
Moderately to take
This sorrow that I make
For Philip Sparrow's sake!
So fervently I shake,
I feel my body quake;
So urgently I am brought
Into careful thought.
Like Andromach, Hector's wife,
Was weary of her life,
When she had lost her joy,   110
Noble Hector of Troy;
In like manner also
Increaseth my deadly woe,
For my sparrow is go[ne].
    It was so pretty a fool,
It would sit on a stool,
And learned after my school
For to keep his cut,
With, 'Philip, keep your cut!'
    It had a velvet cap,   120
And would sit upon my lap,
And seek after small worms,
And sometime white bread crumbs;
And many times and oft
Between my breasts soft
It would lie and rest;
It was proper and prest.
    Sometime he would gasp

When he saw a wasp;
A fly or a gnat,   130
He would fly at that;
And prettily he would pant
When he saw an ant;
Lord, how he would pry
After the butterfly!
Lord, how he would hop
After the gressop!
And when I said, 'Phip, Phip',
Then he would leap and skip,
And take me by the lip.   140
Alas, it will me slay
That Philip is gone me fro!
    Si in i qui ta tes,
Alas, I was evil at ease!
De pro fun dis cla ma vi,
When I saw my sparrow die!
    Now, after my dome,
Dame Sulpicia at Rome,
Whose name registered was
For ever in tables of brass,   150
Because that she did pass
In poesy to indite,
And eloquently to write,
Though she would pretend
My sparrow to commend,
I trow she could not amend
Reporting the virtues all
Of my sparrow royal.
    For it would come and go,
And fly so to and fro;   160
And on me it would leap
When I was asleep,
And his feathers shake,
Wherewith he would make
Me often for to wake,
And for to take him in
Upon my naked skin;
God wot, we thought no sin:

What though he crept so low?
It was no hurt, I trow,   170
He did nothing perde
But sit upon my knee:
Philip, though he were nice,
In him it was no vice;
Philip had leave to go
To pick my little toe;
Philip might be bold
And do what he would;
Philip would seek and take
All the fleas black
That he could there espy   180
With his wanton eye.
     O pe ra,
La, soll, fa, fa,
Confitebor tibi, Domine, in toto corde meo.
Alas, I would ride and go
A thousand mile of ground,
If any such might be found!
It were worth an hundred pound
Of King Cresus' gold,   190
Or of Attalus the old,
The rich prince of Pargame,
Who so list the story to see.
Cadmus, that his sister sought,
And he should be bought
For gold and fee,
He should over the sea,
To wit if he could bring
Any of the offspring,
Or any of the blood.   200
But whoso understood
Of Medea's art,
I would I had a part
Of her crafty magic!
My sparrow then should be quick
With a charm or twain,
And play with me again.
But all this is in vain

Thus for to complain.
  I took my sampler once,   210
Of purpose, for the nonce,
To sew with stitches of silk
My sparrow white as milk,
That by representation
Of his image and fashion,
To me it might import
Some pleasure and comfort
For my solace and sport:
But when I was sewing his beak,
Methought, my sparrow did speak,   220
And opened his pretty bill,
Saying, 'Maid, ye are in will
Against me for to kill,
Ye prick me in the head!'
With that my needle waxed red,
Methought, of Philip's blood;
Mine hair right upstood,
And was in such a fray,
My speech was taken away.
I cast down that there was,   230
And said, 'Alas, alas,
How commeth this to pass?'
My fingers, dead and cold,
Could not my sampler hold;
My needle and thread
I threw away for dread.
The best now that I may,
Is for his soul to pray:
A porta inferi,
Good Lord, have mercy   240
Upon my sparrow's soul,
Written in my bead-roll!
  Au di vi vo cem,
Japhet, Cam, and Sem,
Ma gni fi cat,
Show me the right path
To the hills of Armony,
Wherefore the birds yet cry

Of your father's boat,
That was sometime afloat,   250
And now they die and rot;
Let some poets write
Deucalion's flood it hight:
But as verily as ye be
The natural sons three
Of Noah the patriarch,
That made that great ark,
Wherin he had apes and owls,
Beasts, birds, and fowls,
That if ye can find   260
Any of my sparrow's kind,
God send the soul good rest!
I would have yet a nest
As pretty and as prest
As my sparrow was.
But my sparrow did pass
All sparrows of the wood
That were since Noah's flood,
Was never none so good;
King Philip of Macedony   270
Had no such Philip as I,
No, no, sir, hardly.
    That vengeance I ask and cry,
By way of exclamation,
On all the whole nation,
Of cats wild and tame;
God send them sorrow and shame!
That cat specially
That slew so cruelly
My little pretty sparrow   280
That I brought up at Carrow.
    O cat of carlish kind,
The fiend was in thy mind
When thou my bird untwined!
I would thou haddest been blind!
The leopards savage,
The lions in their rage,
Might catch thee in their paws,

And gnaw thee in their jaws!
The serpents of Libany   290
Might sting thee venomously!
The dragons with their tongues
Might poison thy liver and lungs!
The manticores of the mountains
Might feed them on thy brains!
    Melanchates, that hound
That plucked Acteon to the ground,
Gave him his mortal wound,
Changed to a deer,
The story doth appear,   300
Was changed to an hart:
So thou, foul cat that thou art,
The self-same hound
Might thee confound,
That his own lord bote,
Might bite assunder thy throat!
    Of Inde the greedy gripes
Might tear out all thy tripes!
Of Arcady the bears
Might pluck away thine ears!   310
The wild wolf Lycaon
Bite assunder thy back-bone!
Of Etna the burning hill,
That day and night burneth still,
Set in thy tail a blaze,
That all the world may gaze
And wonder upon thee,
From Occyan the greate sea
Unto the Iles of Orchady,
From Tilbury ferry   320
To the plain of Salisbury!
So traitorously my bird to kill
That never ought thee evil will!
    Was never bird in cage
More gentle of courage
In doing his homage
Unto his sovereign.
Alas, I say again,

Death hath departed us twain!
The false cat hath thee slain: 330
Farewell, Philip, adieu!
Our Lord thy soul rescue!
Farewell without restore,
Farewell for evermore!
　　And it were a Jew,
It would make one rue,
To see my sorrow new.
These villainous false cats
Were made for mice and rats,
And not for birds small.   340
Alas, my face waxeth pale,
Telling this piteous tale,
How my bird so fair,
That was wont to repair,
And go in at my spaire,
And creep in at my gore
Of my gown before,
Flickering with his wings!
Alas, my heart it stings,
Remembering pretty things!   350
Alas, mine heart it slayeth
My Philip's doleful death,
When I remember it,
How prettily it would sit,
Many times and oft,
Upon my finger aloft!
I played with him tittle tattle,
And fed him with my spittle,
With his bill between my lips;
It was my pretty Phips!   360
Many a pretty kiss
Had I of his sweet musse;
And now the cause is thus,
That he is slain me fro,
To my great pain and woe.
　　Of fortune this the chance
Standeth on variance:
Oft time after pleasance

Trouble and grievance;
No man can be sure   370
Always to have pleasure:
As well perceive ye may
How my desport and play
From me was taken away
By Gib, our cat savage,
That in a furious rage
Caught Philip by the head,
And slew him there stark dead.
  Kyrie, eleison,
  Christe, eleison,   380
  Kyrie, eleison!
For Philip Sparrow's soul,
Set in our bead-roll,
Let us now whisper
A *Pater noster.*
 Lauda, anima mea, Dominum!
To weep with me look that ye come,
All manner of birds in your kind;
Se none be left behind.
To mourning look that ye fall   390
With dolorous songs funeral,
Some to sing, and some to say,
Some to weep, and some to pray,
Every bird in his lay.
The goldfinch, the wagtail;
The jangling jay to rail,
The flecked pie to chatter
Of this dolorous matter;
And robin redbreast,
He shall be the priest   400
The requiem mass to sing,
Softly warbling,
With help of the red sparrow,
And the chattering swallow,
This hearse for to hallow;
The lark with his long toe;
The spink, and the martinet also;
The shoveller with his broad beak;

The doterell, that foolish peak,
And also the mad coot,   410
With a bald face to toot;
The fieldfare, and the snite;
The crow, and the kite;
The raven, called Rolfe,
His plain-song to solfe;
The partridge, the quail;
The plover with us to wail;
The woodhack, that singeth 'chur'
Hoarsely, as he had the mur;
The lusty chanting nightingale;   420
The popingay to tell her tale,
That toteth oft in a glass,
Shall read the Gospel at mass;
The mavis with her whistle
Shall read there the Epistle.
But with a large and a long
To keep just plain-song,
Our chanters shall be the cuckoo,
The culver, the stockdove,
With peewit the lapwing,   430
The versicles shall sing.
    The bittern with his bump,
The crane with his trump,
The swan of Menander,
The goose and the gander,
The duck and the drake,
Shall watch at this wake;
The peacock so proud,
Because his voice is loud,
And hath a glorious tail,   440
He shall sing the grail;
The owl, that is so foul,
Must help us to howl;
The heron so gaunt,
And the cormorant,
With the pheasant,
And the gaggling gaunt,
And the churlish chough;

The route and the cough;
The barnacle, the buzzard,   450
With the wild mallard:
The divendop to sleep;
The water hen to weep;
The puffin and the teal
Money they shall deal
To poor folk at large,
That shall be their charge;
The seamew and the titmouse;
The woodcock with the long nose;
The throstle with her warbling;   460
The starling with her babbling;
The rook, with the osprey
That putteth fishes to a fray;
And the dainty curlew,
With the turtle most true.
    At this *Placebo*
We may not well forgo
The countering of the coe:
The stork also,
That maketh his nest   470
In chimneys to rest;
Within those walls
No broken galls
May there abide
Of cuckoldry side,
Or else philosophy
Maketh a great lie.
    The ostrich, that will eat
An horseshoe so great,
In the stead of meat,   480
Such fervent heat
His stomach doth fret;
He cannot well fly,
Nor sing tunably,
Yet at a braid
He hath well assayed
To solfe above 'ela',
Ga, lorell, fa, fa;

Ne quando
Male cantando,   490
The best that we can,
To make him our bellman,
And let him ring the bells;
He can do nothing else.
      Chanteclere, our cock,
Must tell what is of the clock
By the astrology
That he hath naturally
Conceived and caught,
And was never tought   500
By Albumazer
The astronomer,
Nor by Ptholomy
Prince of astronomy,
Nor yet by Haly;
And yet he croweth daily
And nightly the tides
That no man abides,
With Partlot his hen,
Whom now and then   510
He plucketh by the head
When he doth her tread.
      The bird of Araby,
That potentially
May never die,
And yet there is none
But one alone;
A phoenix it is
This hearse that must bless
With aromatic gums   520
That cost great sums,
The way of thurification
To make a fumigation,
Sweat of reflary,
And redolent of air,
This corpse for to cense
With great reverence,
As patriarch or pope

In a black cope;
Whiles he censeth [the hearse],   530
He shall sing the verse,
Libera me,
In *de*, *la*, *soll*, *re*,
Softly bemole
For my sparrow's soul.
Pliny showeth all
In his story natural
What he doth find
Of the phoenix kind;
Of whose incineration   540
There riseth a new creation
Of the same fashion
Without alteration,
Saying that old age
Is turned into courage
Of fresh youth again;
This matter true and plain,
Plain matter indeed,
Who so list to read.
   But for the eagle doth fly   550
Highest in the sky,
He shall be the sedean,
The choir to demean,
As provost principal,
To teach them their ordinal;
Also the noble falcon,
With the gerfalcon,
The tercel gentle,
They shall mourn soft and still
In their amice of grey;   560
The sacre with them shall say
Dirige for Philip's soul;
The goshawk shall have a role
The choristers to control;
The lanners and the marlions
Shall stand in their morning gowns;
The hobby and the muskett
The censers and the cross shall fetch;

The kestrel in all this work
Shall be holy water clerk.   570
    And now the dark cloudy night
Chaseth away Phoebus bright,
Taking his course toward the west,
God send my sparrow's soul good rest!
Requiem æternam dona eis, Domine!
Fa, fa, fa, my, re, re,
A por ta in fe ri,
Fa, fa, fa, my, my.
    Credo videre bona Domini,
I pray God, Philip to heaven may fly!   580
Domine, exaudi oractionem meam!
To Heaven he shall, from heaven he came!
    Do mi nus vo bis cum!
Of all good prayers God send him [the] sum!
       Oremus.
Deus, cui proprium est miserere et parcere,
On Philip's soul have pity!
For he was a pretty cock,
And came of a gentle stock,
And wrapped in a maiden's smock,   590
And cherished full daintily,
Till cruel fate made him to die:
Alas, for doleful destiny!
But whereto should I
Longer mourn or cry?
To Jupiter I call,
Of heaven imperial,
That Philip may fly
Above the starry sky,
To tread the pretty wren,   600
That is our Lady's hen:
Amen, amen, amen!
    Yet one thing is behind,
That now commeth to mind;
An epitaph I would have
For Philip's grave:
But for I am a maid,
Timorous, half afraid,

That never yet assayed
Of Helicon's well,   610
Where the Muses dwell;
Though I can read and spell,
Recount, report, and tell
Of the Tales of Canterbury,
Some sad stories, some merry;
As Palamon and Arcet,
Duke Theseus, and Partelet;
And of the Wife of Bath,
That worketh much scath
When her tale is told   620
Among housewives bold,
How she controlled
Her husbands as she would,
And them to despise
In the homliest wise,
Bring other wives in thought
Their husbands to set at nought:
And though that read have I
Of Gawain and Sir Guy,
And tell can a great piece   630
Of the Golden Fleece,
How Jason it won,
Like a valiant man;
Of Arthur's round table,
With his knights commendable,
And Dame Guinevere, his queen,
Was somewhat wanton, I wene:
How Sir Lancelot de Lake
Many a spear break
For his lady's sake;   640
Of Tristram, and King Mark,
And all the whole work
Of Belle Isold his wife,
For whom was much strife;
Some say she was light,
And made her husband knight
Of the common hall,
That cuckolds men call;

And of Sir Lybius,
Named Dysconius;   650
Of *Quater Fylz Amund*,
And how they were summoned
To Rome, to Charlemagne,
Upon a great pain,
And how they rode each one
On Bayard Mountalbon;
Men see him now and then
In the forest of Arden:
What though I can frame
The stories by name   660
Of Judas Maccabeus,
And of Caesar Julius:
And of the love between
Paris and Vienne;
And of the duke Hannibal,
That made the Romans all
Fordread and to quake;
How Scipion did wake
The city of Carthage,
Which by his unmerciful rage   670
He beat down to the ground:
And though I can expound
Of Hector of Troy,
That was all their joy,
Whom Achilles slew,
Wherefore all Troy did rue;
And of the love so hot
That made Troilus to dote
Upon fair Cressyde,
And what they wrote and said,   680
And of their wanton wiles
Pandar bare the bills
From one to the other;
His master's love to further,
Sometime a precious thing,
An ouche, or else a ring;
From her to him again
Sometime a pretty chain,

Or a bracelet of her hair,
Prayed Troilus for to wear   690
That token for her sake;
How heartily he did it take,
And much therof did make;
And all that was in vain,
For she did but fain;
The story telleth plain,
He could not obtain,
Though his father were a king
Yet there was a thing
That made the male to wring;   700
She made him to sing
The song of lovers lay;
Musing night and day,
Mourning all alone,
Comfort had he none,
For she was quite gone;
Thus in conclusion,
She brought him in abusion;
In earnest and in game
She was much to blame;   710
Disparaged is her fame,
And blemished is her name,
In manner half with shame;
Troilus also hath lost
On her much love and cost,
And now must kiss the post;
Pandar, that went between,
Hath won nothing, I wene,
But light for summer green;
Yet for a special laud   720
He is named Troilus bawd,
Of that name he is sure
While the world shall endure:
    Though I remember the fable
Of Penelope most stable,
To her husband most true,
Yet long time she ne knew
Whether he were alive or dead;

Her wit stood her in stead,
That she was true and just   730
For any bodily lust
To Ulysses her mate,
And never would him forsake:
    Of Marcus Marcellus
A process I could tell us;
And of Anteocus;
And of Josephus
De Antiquitatibus;
And of Mardocheus,
And of great Assuerus,   740
And of Vesca his queen,
Whom he forsook with teen,
And of Hester his other wife,
With whom he led a pleasant life;
Of King Alexander;
And of King Evander;
And of Porcena the great,
That made the Romans to sweat:
    Though I have enrolled
A thousand new and old   750
Of these historious tales,
To fill bougets and males
With books that I have read,
Yet I am nothing sped,
And can but little skill
Of Ovid or Virgil,
Or of Plutarch,
Or Francis Petrarch,
Alcheus or Sappho,
Or such other poets mo,   760
As Linus and Homerus,
Euphorion and Theocritus,
Anacreon and Arion,
Sophocles and Philemon,
Pindarus and Simonides,
Philistion and Phorocides;
These poets of ancient,
They are too diffuse for me:

For, as I tofore have said,
I am but a young maid,   770
And cannot in effect
My style as yet direct
With English words elect:
Our natural tongue is rude,
And hard to be ennewed
With polished terms lusty;
Our language is so rusty,
So cankered, and so full
Of frowards, and so dull,
That if I would apply   780
To write ornately,
I wot not where to find
Terms to serve my mind.
   Gower's English is old,
And of no value told;
His matter is worth gold,
And worthy to be enrolled.
   In Chaucer I am sped,
His tales I have read:
His matter is delectable,   790
Solacious, and commendable;
His English well allowed,
So as it is enprowed,
For as it is employed,
There is no English void,
At those days much commended,
And now men would have amended
His English, whereat they bark,
And mar all they work:
Chaucer, that famous clerk,   800
His terms were not dark,
But pleasant, easy, and plain;
No word he wrote in vain.
   Also John Lydgate
Writeth after an higher rate;
It is diffused to find
The sentence of his mind,
Yet writeth he in his kind,

No man that can amend
Those matters that he hath penned;　　　810
Yet some men find a fault,
And say he writeth too haught.
　　Wherefore hold me excused
If I have not well perused
Mine English half abused;
Though it be refused,
In worth I shall it take,
And fewer words make.
　　But, for my sparrow's sake,
Yet as a woman may,　　　820
My wit I shall assay
An epitaph to write
In Latin plain and light,
Whereof the elegy
Followeth by and by:
Flos volucrum formose, vale!
Philippe, sub isto
Marmore jam recubas,
Qui mihi carus eras
Semper erunt nitido　　　830
Radiantia sidera cœlo;
Impressusque meo
Pectore semper eris. [. . .]

THE COMMENDATIONS

Beati im ma cu la ti in via,
O gloriosa fœmina!
Now mine whole imagination
And studious meditation
Is to take this commendation
In this consideration;　　　850
And under patient toleration
Of that most goodly maid
That *Placebo* hath said,
And for her sparrow prayed
In lamentable wise,
Now will I enterprise,
Through the grace divine

Of the Muses nine,
Her beauty to commend,
If Arethusa will send   860
Me influence to indict,
And with my pen to write;
If Apollo will promise
Melodiously it to devise
His tunable harp strings
With harmony that sings
Of princes and of kings
And of all pleasant things,
Of lust and of delight,
Through his godly might;   870
To whom be the laud ascribed
That my pen hath imbibed
With the aureate drops,
As verily my hope is,
Of Tagus, that golden flood,
That passeth all earthly good;
And as that flood doth pass
All floods that ever was
With his golden sands,
Who so that understands   880
Cosmography, and the streams
And the floods in strange realms,
Right so she doth exceed
All other of whom we read,
Whose fame by me shall spread
Into Persia and Media,
From Britain's Albion
To the Tower of Babylon. [. . .]
    How shall I report
All the goodly sort
Of her features clear,   1000
That hath no earthly peer?
Her favour of her face
Ennewed all with grace,
Comfort, pleasure, and solace,
Mine heart doth so embrace,
And so hath ravished me

Her to behold and see,
That in words plain
I cannot me refrain
To look on her again: 1010
Alas, what should I fain?
It were a pleasant pain
With her aye to remain.
　　Her eyes grey and steep
Causeth mine heart to leap;
With her brows bent
She may well represent
Fair Lucres, as I wene,
Or else fair Polexene,
Or else Caliope,   1020
Or else Penelope;
For this most goodly flower,
This blossom of fresh colour,
So Jupiter me succour,
She flourisheth new and new
In beauty and virtue:
Hac claritate gemina
O gloriosa fœmina,
Memor esto verbi tui servo tuo!
Servus tuus sum ego.   1030
　　The Inde sapphire blue
Her veins doth ennew;
The orient pearl so clear,
The whiteness of her lere;
The lusty ruby ruds
Resemble the rose buds;
Her lips soft and merry
Embloomed like the cherry,
It were an heavenly bliss
Her sugared mouth to kiss.   1040
　　Her beauty to augment,
Dame Nature hath her lent
A wart upon her cheek,
Who so list to seek
In her visage a scar,
That seemeth from afar

Like to the radiant star,
All with favour fret,
So properly it is set:
She is the violet,   1050
The daisy delectable,
The columbine commendable,
The gillyflower amiable;
[For] this most goodly flower,
This blossom of fresh colour,
So Jupiter me succour,
She flourisheth new and new
In beauty and virtue:
Hac claritate gemina
O gloriosa fœmina,   1060
Bonitatem fecisti cum servo tuo, domina,
Et ex prœcordiis sonant prœconia!
    And when I perceived
Her wart and conceived,
It cannot be denied
But it was well conveyed,
And set so womanly,
And nothing wantonly,
But right conveniently,
And full congruently,   1070
As Nature could devise
In most goodly wise;
Who so list behold,
It maketh lovers bold
To her to sue for grace,
Her favour to purchase;
The scar upon her chin,
Enhatched on her fair skin,
Whiter than the swan,
It would make any man   1080
To forget deadly sin
Her favour to win:
For this most goodly flower,
This blossom of fresh colour,
So Jupiter me succour,
She flourisheth new and new

In beauty and virtue:
Hac claritate gemina
O gloriosa fœmina,
Defecit in salutare tuum tua anima mea; 1090
Quid petis filio, mater dulcissima? baba!
   Soft, and make no din,
For now I will begin
To have in remembrance
Her goodly dalliance,
And her goodly pastance:
So sad and so demure,
Behaving her so sure,
With words of pleasure
She would make to the lure 1100
And any man convert
To give her his whole heart.
She made me sore amazed
Upon her when I gazed,
Me thought mine heart was crazed,
My eyes were so dazed;
For this most goodly flower,
This blossom of fresh colour,
So Jupiter me succour,
She flourisheth new and new 1110
In beauty and virtue:
Hac claritate gemina
O gloriosa fœmina,
Quomodo dilexi legem tuam, domina!
Recedant vetera, nova sunt omnia.
   And to amend her tale,
When she list to avail,
And with her fingers small,
And hands soft as silk,
Whiter than the milk, 1120
That are so quickly veined,
Wherewith my hand she strained,
Lord, how I was pained!
Unneth I me refrained,
How she me had reclaimed,
And me to her retained,

Embracing therewithall
Her goodly middle small
With sides long and straight;
To tell you what conceit   1130
I had then in a trice,
The matter were too nice,
And yet there was no vice,
Nor yet no villainy,
But only fantasy;
For this most goodly flower,
This blossom of fresh colour,
So Jupiter me succour,
She flourisheth new and new
In beauty and virtue: 1140
Hac claritate gemina
O gloriosa fœmina,
Iniquos odio habui!
Non calumnientur me superbi.
   But whereto should I note
How often did I tote
Upon her pretty foot?
It raised my heart root
To see her tread the ground
With heels short and round.   1150
She is plainly express
Egeria, the goddess,
And like to her image,
Emportured with courage,
A lover's pilgrimage;
There is no beast savage,
Ne no tiger so wood,
But she would change his mood,
Such relucent grace
Is formed in her face;   1160
For this most goodly flower,
This blossom of fresh colour,
So Jupiter me succour,
She flourisheth new and new
In beauty and virtue:
Hac claritate gemina

O gloriosa fœmina,
Mirabilia testimonia tua!
Sicut novellæ plantationes in juventute sua.
　　So goodly as she dresses,   1170
So properly she presses
The bright golden tresses
Of her hair so fine,
Like Phoebus beams shine.
Wherto should I disclose
The gartering of her hose?
It is for to suppose
How that she can wear
Gorgeously her gear;
Her fresh habilments   1180
With other implements
To serve for all intents,
Like Dame Flora, queen
Of lusty summer green;
For this most goodly flower,
This blossom of fresh colour,
So Jupiter me succour,
She flourisheth new and new
In beauty and virtue:
Hac claritate gemina   1190
O gloriosa fœmina,
Clamavi in toto corde, exaudi me!
Misericordia tua magna est super me.
Her kirtle so goodly laced,
And under that is braced
Such pleasures that I may
Neither write nor say;
Yet though I write not with ink,
No man can let me think,
For thought hath liberty,   1200
Thought is frank and free;
To think a merry thought
It cost me little or nought.
Would God mine homely style
Were polished with the file
Of Cicero's eloquence,

To praise her excellence!
For this most goodly flower,
This blossom of fresh colour,
So Jupiter me succour,   1210
She flourisheth new and new
In beauty and virtue:
Hac claritate gemina
O gloriosa fœmina,
Principes persecuti sunt me gratis!
Omnibus consideratis,
Paradisus voluptatis
Hœc virgo est dulcissima.
  My pen it is unable,   1220
My hand it is unstable
My reason rude and dull
To praise her at the full;
Goodly mistress Jane,
Sober, demure Diane;
Jane this mistress hight
The lode star of delight,
Dame Venus of all pleasure,
The well of worldly treasure;
She doth exceed and pass
In prudence Dame Pallas;   1230
[For] this most goodly flower,
This blossom of fresh colour,
So Jupiter me succour,
She flourisheth new and new
In beauty and virtue:
Hac claritate gemina
O gloriosa fœmina!
  Requiem œternam dona eis, Domine!
With this psalm, *Domine, probasti me,*
Shall sail over the sea,   1240
With *Tibi, Domine, commendamus,*
On pilgrimage to Saint James,
For shrimps, and for prawns,
And for stalking cranes;
And where my pen hath offended,
I pray you it may be amended

By discreet consideration
Of your wise reformation;
I have not offended, I trust,
If it be sadly discussed. 1250
It were no gentle guise
This treatise to despise
Because I have written and said
Honour to this fair maid;
Wherefore should I be blamed,
That I Jane have named,
And famously proclaimed?
She is worthy to be enrolled
With letters of gold. [. . .]

Elynour Rummyng

Tell you I chill,
If that ye will
A while be still,
Of a comely girl
That dwelt on a hill:
But she is not grill,
For she is somewhat sage
And well worn in age;
For her visage
It would assuage 10
A man's courage.

　Her loathly lere
Is nothing clear,
But ugly of cheer,
Droopy and drowsy,
Scurvy and lousy;
Her face all bowsy,
Comely crinkled,
Wondrously wrinkled,
Like a roast pig's ear, 20

Bristled with hair.
   Her lewd lips twain,
They slaver, men sayn,
Like a ropy rain,
A gummy glare:
She is ugly fair;
Her nose somedeal hooked,
And camously crooked,
Never stopping,
But ever dropping;   30
Her skin loose and slack,
Grained like a sack;
With a crooked back.
   Her eyen gowndy
Are full unsoundy,
For they are bleared;
And she grey-haired;
Jawed like a jetty;
A man would have pity
To see how she is gummed,   40
Fingered and thumbed,
Gently jointed,
Greased and annointed
Up to the knuckles;
The bones [of] her huckels
Like as they were with buckles
Together made fast:
Her youth is far passed:
Footed like a plane,
Legged like a crane;   50
And yet she will jet,
Like a jolly fet,
In her furred flocket,
And grey russet rocket,
With simper the cocket.
Her hood of Lincoln green,
It has been hers, I wene,
More than forty year;
And so doth it appear,
For the green bare threads   60

Look like sere weeds,
Withered like hay,
The wool worn away;
And yet I dare say
She thinketh herself gay
Upon the holy day,
When she doth her array,
And girdeth in her gites
Stitched and pranked with pleats;
Her kirtle Bristol red,   70
With clothes upon her head
That weigh a sow of lead,
Writhen in wonder wise,
After the Saracen's guise,
With a whim-wham,
Knit with a trim-tram,
Upon her brain pan,
Like an Egyptian,
Capped about:
When she goeth out   80
Herself for to show,
She driveth down the dew
With a pair of heels
As broad as two wheels;
She hobbles as a goose
With her blanket hose
Over the fallow;
Her shoes smeared with tallow,
Greased upon dirt
That baudeth her skirt.   90

Primus passus
And this comely dame,
I understand, her name
Is Elynour Rummyng,
At home in her wonning;
And as men say
She dwelt in Surrey,
In a certain stead
Beside Leatherhead.

She is a tunnish gib;
The devil and she be sib.   100
   But to make up my tale,
She breweth noppy ale,
And maketh therof port sale
To travellers, to tinkers,
To sweaters, to swinkers,
And all good ale drinkers,
That will nothing spare,
But drink till they stare
And bring themself bare,
With, 'Now away the mare,   110
And let us slay care',
As wise as an hare!
   Come who so will
To Elynour on the hill,
With, 'Fill the cup, fill',
And sit there by still,
Early and late:
Thither cometh Kate,
Cicely, and Sarah,
With their legs bare,   120
And also their feet
Hardely full unsweet;
With their heel dagged,
Their kirtles all to-jagged,
Their smocks all to-ragged,
With titters and tatters,
Bring dishes and platters,
With all their might running
To Elynour Rummyng,
To have of her tunning: 130
She leaneth them on the same,
And thus beginneth the game.
   Some wenches come unlaced,
Some housewives come unbraced,
With their naked paps,
That flips and flaps;
It wigs and it wags,
Like tawny saffron bags;

A sort of foul drabs
All scurvy with scabs: 140
Some be flybitten,
Some skewed as a kitten;
Some with a shoe clout
Bind their heads about;
Some have no hair-lace,
Their locks about their face,
Their tresses untrust,
All full of unlust;
Some look strawy,
Some cawry-mawry;   150
Full untidy teggs,
Like rotten eggs.
Such a lewd sort
To Elynour resort
From tide to tide:
Abide, abide,
And to you shall be told
How her ale is sold
To malt and to mould.

Secundus passus

Some have no money   160
That thither commy,
For their ale to pay,
That is a shrewd array;
Elynour sweared, 'Nay,
Ye shall not bear away
My ale for nought,
By Him that me bought!'
  With, 'Hey, dog, hey,
Have these hogs away!'
With, 'Get me a staff,   170
The swine eat my draff!'
'Strike the hogs with a club,
They have drunk up my swilling tub!'
For, be there never so much press,
These swine go to the high dais,
The sow with her pigs;

The boar his tail wrigs,
His rump also he frigs
Against the high bench!
With, 'Fo, there is a stench!'   180
Gather up, thou wench;
Seest thou not what is fall?
Take up dirt and all,
And bear out of the hall;
God give it ill preving,
Cleanly as evil cheving!
    But let us turn plain,
There we left again.
For, as ill a patch as that,
The hens run in the mashfat;   190
For they go to roost
Straight over the ale joust,
And dung, when it comes,
In the ale tuns.
Then Elynour taketh
The mash-bowl, and shaketh
The hens dung away,
And skimmeth it into a tray
Whereas the yeast is,
With her mangy fists: 200
And sometime she blends
The dung of her hens
And the ale together;
And sayeth, 'Gossip, come hither,
This ale shall be thicker,
And flower the more quicker;
For I may tell you,
I learned it of a Jew,
When I began to brew,
And I have found it true;   210
Drink now while it is new;
And ye may it broke,
It shall make you look
Younger than ye be
Years two or three,
For ye may prove it by me';

'Behold,' she said, 'and see
How bright I am of blee!
I am not cast away,
That can my husband say,   220
When we kiss and play
In lust and in liking;
He calleth me his whiting,
His mulling and his miting,
His nobs and his coney,
His sweeting and his honey,
With, "Bas, my pretty bonny,
Thou art worth good and monny."
This make I my fellow fonny,
Till that he dream and dronny;   230
For, after all our sport,
Then will he rout and snort;
Then sweetely together we lie,
As two pigs in a sty.'

   To cease me seemeth best,
And of this tale to rest,
And for to leave this letter,
Because it is no better,
And because it is no sweeter;
We will no farther rhyme   240
Of it at this time;
But we will turn plain
Where we left again.

Tertius passus
   Instead of coin and money,
Some bring her a coney,
And some a pot with honey,
Some a salt, and some a spoon,
Some their hose, some their shoon;
Some run a good trot
With a skillet or a pot;   250
Some fill their pot full
Of good Lemster wool:
A housewife of trust,
When she is athrust,

Such a web can spin,
Her thrift is full thin.
   Some go straight thither,
Be it slaty or slidder;
They hold the high-way,
They care not what men say,   260
Be that as be may;
Some, loath to be espied,
Start in at the back side,
Over the hedge and pale,
And all for the good ale.
   Some run till they sweat,
Bring with them malt or wheat,
And dame Elynour entreat
To birl them of the best.
   Then cometh another guest;   270
She swears by the rood of rest,
Her lips are so dry,
Without drink she must die;
Therefore fill it by and by,
And have here a peck of rye.
   Anon cometh another,
As dry as the other,
And with her doth bring
Meal, salt, or other thing,
Her harvest-girdle, her wedding ring,   280
To pay for her scot
As cometh to her lot.
Some bringeth her husband's hood,
Because the ale is good;
Another brought her his cap
To offer to the ale tap,
With flax and with tow;
And some brought sour dough;
With, 'Hey', and with 'how',
Sit we down a row,   290
And drink till we blow,
And pipe tirly-tirlowe!
   Some laid to pledge
Their hatchet and their wedge,

Their hekell and their reel,
Their rock, their spinning wheel;
And some went so narrow,
They laid to pledge their wharrow,
Their ribskin and their spindle,
Their needle and their thimble: 300
Here was scant thrift
When they made such shift.

   Their thirst was so great,
They asked never for meat
But drink, still drink,
And let the cat wink,
Let us wash our gums
From the dry crumbs.

Quartus passus
   Some for very need
Lay down a skein of thread,   310
And some a skein of yarn;
Some brought from the barn
Both beans and peas;
Small chaffer doth ease
Sometime, now and then:
Another there was that ran
With a good brass pan;
Her colour was full wan;
She ran in all the haste
Unbraced and unlaced;   320
Tawny, swart, and sallow,
Like a cake of tallow;
I swear by All Hallow,
It was a stale to take
The devil in a brake.

   And then came halting Joan,
And brought a gammon
Of bacon that was resty:
But, Lord, as she was testy,
Angry as a wasp!   330
She began to yawn and gasp,
And bad Elynour go bet,

And fill in good met;
It was dear that was far-fetched.
   Another brought a spick
Of a bacon flitch;
Her tongue was very quick,
But she spake somewhat thick:
Her fellow did stammer and stut,
But she was a foul slut, 340
For her mouth foamed
And her belly groaned:
Joan said she had eaten a fiest;
'By Christ,' said she, 'thou liest,
I have as sweet a breath
As thou, with shameful death!'
   Then Elynour said, 'Ye calletts,
I shall break your paletts,
Without ye now cease!'
And so was made the peace. 350
   Then thither came drunken Alice;
And she was full of tales,
Of tidings in Wales,
And of Saint James in Gales,
And of the Portingales;
With, 'Lo, gossip, I wis,
Thus and thus it is,
There hath been great war
Between Temple Bar
And the Cross in Cheap, 360
And there came an heap
Of millstones in a route:
She speaketh thus in her snout,
Snivelling in her nose,
As though she had the pose;
Lo, here is an old tippet,
And ye will give me a snippet
Of your stale ale,
God send you good sale!
And as she was drinking, 370
She fell in a winking
With a barleyhood,

She pissed where she stood;
Then began she to weep,
And forthwith fell on sleep.
Elynour took her up,
And blessed her with a cup
Of new ale in corns;
Alice found therin no thorns,
But supped it up at once,   380
She found therin no bones. [. . .]

Septimus passus
'Soft,' quod one hight Sybil,
'And let me with you bibble.'   550
She sat down in the place,
With a sorry face
Wheywormed about;
Garnished was her snout
With her and there a pustule,
Like a scabbed mussel.
'This ale,' said she, 'is noppy;
Let us sip and sop,
And not spill a drop,
For so moot I hop,   560
It cooleth well my crop.'
   'Dame Elynour,' said she,
'Have here is for me,
A clout of London pins;'
And with that she begins
The pot to her pluck,
And drank a good luck;
She swinged up a quart
At once for her part;
Her paunch was so puffed,   570
And so with ale stuffed,
Had she not hied apace,
She had defiled the place.
   Then began the sport
Among that drunken sort:
'Dame Elynour,' said they,
'Lend here a cock of hay,

To make all thing clean;
Ye woot well what we mean.'
   But, sir, among all   580
That sat in that hall,
There was a pryckemedenty,
Sat like a sentry,
And began to pant,
As though she would faint;
She made it as coy
As a *lege de moy*;
She was not half so wise
As she was peevish-nice.
She said never a word,   590
But rose from the board,
And called for our dame,
Elynour by name.
We supposed, I wis,
That she rose to piss;
But the very ground
Was for to compound
With Elynour in the spence,
To pay for her expense:
'I have no penny nor groat   600
To pay,' said she, 'God wote,
For washing of my throat;
But my beads of amber
Bear them to your chamber.'
Then Elynour did them hide
Within her bed's side.
   But some then sat right sad
That nothing had
There of their own,
Neither gilt nor pawn;   610
Such were there many
That had not a penny,
But, when they should walk,
Were fain with a chalk
To score on the balk,
Or score on the tail:

God give it ill-hail!
For my fingers itch;
I have written too mitch
Of this mad mumming   620
Of Elynour Rummyng.
Thus endeth the jest
Of this worthy fest.

Against Garnesche

I have your lewd letter received,
And well I have it perceived,
And your scribe I have aspied,
That your mad mind contrived.
Saving your usher's rod,
I cast me not to be odd
With neither of you twain:
Wherefore I write again;
How the favour of your face
Is void of all good grace;   10
For all your carpet cushions,
Ye have knavish conditions.
Gup, marmoset, jast ye, morell!
I am laureat, I am no lorell.
Lewdly your time ye spend,
My living to reprehend;
And will never intend
Your own lewdness to amend:
Your English lew[d]ly ye sort,
And falsely ye me report.   20
Garnesche, ye gape too wide:
Your knavery I will nat hide,
For to assuage your pride.
 When ye were younger of age,
Ye were a kitchen page,
A dishwasher, a drivel,

In the pot your nose did snivel;
Ye fried and ye broiled,
Ye roasted and ye boiled,
Ye roasted, like a fonne,   30
A goose with the feet upon;
Ye sluffered up sauce
In my lady Brews's house.
Wherto should I write
Of such a greasy knight?
A bawdy dishclout,
That bringeth the world about
With hafting and with polling,
With lying and controlling.
    At Guisnes when ye were   40
But a slender spear,
Decked lewdly in your gear;
For when ye dwelt there,
Ye had a knavish coat
Was scantly worth a groat;
In dud frese ye were shrined,
With better frese lined;
The outside every day,
Ye might no better a way;
The inside ye did call   50
Your best gown festival.
Your drapery ye did want,
The ward with you was scant.
When ye cast a sheep's eye,
. . . mistress Andelby,
. . . Guisnes upon a gong,
. . . sat somewhat too long;
. . . her husband's head,
. . . malle of lead,
. . . that ye there preached,   60
To her love ye nought reached:
Ye would have bassed her bum,
So that she would have come
On to your lousy den;
But she of all men
Had you most in despite,

Ye lost her favour quite;
Your pilled garlic head
Could occupy there no stead;
She called you Sir Guy of Gaunt,   70
Nosed like an elephant,
A pikes or a twibill;
She said how ye did bridle,
Much like a dromedary;
Thus with you she did weary,
With much matter more
That I keep in store.
   Your breath is strong and quick;
Ye are an elder-stick;
Ye woot what I think;   80
At both ends ye stink;
Great danger for the king,
When his grace is fasting,
His presence to approach:
It is to your reproach.
It falleth for no swine
Nor sowters to drink wine,
Nor such a noddypoll
A priest for to control.
   Little wit in your scribe's noll   90
That scribbled your fond scroll,
Upon him for to take
Against me for to make,
Like a doctor dawpate,
A laureate poet for to rate.
Your terms are too gross,
Too far from the purpose,
To contaminate
And to violate
The dignity laureate.   100
   Bold Bayard, ye are too blind,
And grow all out of kind,
To occupy so your mind;
For reason can I none find
Nor good rhyme in your matter:
I wonder that ye smatter,

So for a knave to clatter;
Ye would be called a maker,
And make much like Jack Raker;
Ye are a comely craker,   110
Ye learned of some pie-baker.
Cast up your curious writing,
And your dirty indicting,
And your spiteful despiting,
For all is not worth a miting,
A mackerel nor a whiting:
Had ye gone with me to school,
And occupied no better your tool,
Ye should have counted me a fool.
    But now, gawdy, greasy Garnesche,   120
Your face I wish to varnish
So surely it shall not tarnish.
Though a Saracen's head ye bear,
Row and full of lousy hair,
As every man well seeth,
Full of great knave's teeth,
In a field of green peason
Is rhyme yet out of reason;
Your wit is so geson,
Ye rail all out of season.   130
    Your skin scabbed and scurvy,
Tawny, tanned, and shurvy;
Now upon this heat
Rankly when ye sweat,
Men say ye will wax lousy,
Drunken, droopy, drowsy.
Your sword ye swear, I wene,
So trenchant and so keen,
Shall cut both white and green:
Your folly is to great   140
The king's colours to threat.
Your breath it is so fell
And so puauntly doth smell,
And so heinously doth stink,
That neither pump nor sink
Doth savour half so sour

Against a stormy shower.
O ladies of bright colour,
Of beauty that beareth the flower,
When Garnesche cometh you among   150
With his breath so strong,
Without ye have a confection
Against his poisoned infection,
Else with his stinking jaws
He will cause you cast your craws,
And make your stomach sick
Over the perk to prick.
   Now, Garnesche, guard thy gums;
My serpentins and my guns
Against ye now I bind;   160
Thyself therefore defend.
Thou toad, thou scorpion,
Thou bawdy baboon,
Thou bear, thou bristled boar,
Thou moorish manticore,
Thou rammish stinking goat,
Thou foul churlish parrot,
Thou grisly gorgon glaimy,
Thou sweaty sloven seamy,
Thou murrion, thou mawment,   170
Thou false stinking serpent,
Thou mockish marmoset,
I will not die in thy debt.
Tyburn thou me assigned,
Where thou shouldst have been shrined;
The next halter there shall be
I bequeath it whole to thee:
Such pelfry thou hast patched,
And so thyself over-watched
That there thou shouldst be racked,   180
If thou were meetly matched.
   Ye may well be bedawed,
Ye are a fool outlawed;
And for to tell the ground,
Pay Stokes his five pound.
I say, Sir Dalyrag,

Ye bear you bold and brag
With other men's charge:
Ye cut your cloth too large:
Such polling pageants ye play,   190
To point you fresh and gay.
    And he that scribbled your scrolls,
I reckon you in my rolls,
For two drunken souls.
Read and learn ye may,
How old proverbs say,
That bird is not honest
That fouleth his own nest.
If he wist what some woot,
The flesh basting of his coat   200
Was sewed with slender thread:
God send you well good spead,
With *Dominus vobiscum!*
Good Latin for Jake a Thrum,
Till more matter may come.

By the king's most noble commandment.

Speak, Parrot

My name is Parrot, a bird of Paradise,
By Nature devised of a wondrous kind,
Daintily dieted with divers delicate spice,
Till Eufrates, that flood, driveth me into Inde,
Where men of that country by fortune me find,
And send me to great ladies of estate;
Then Parrot must have an almond or a date.

A cage curiously carven, with silver pin,
Properly painted to be my coverture;
A mirror of glass, that I may tote therein;   10
These maidens full merrily with many a divers flower
Freshly they dress and make sweet my bower,

With, 'Speak, Parrot, I pray you,' full courteously they say,
'Parrot is a goodly bird and a pretty popagay.'

With my beak bent, and my little wanton eye,
My feathers fresh as is the emerald green,
About my neck a circulet like the rich ruby,
My little legs, my feet both fete and clean,
I am a minion to wait upon a queen;
'My proper Parrot, my little pretty fool.'   20
With ladies I learn and go with them to school.

'Hee hee, ha, ha, Parrot, ye can laugh prettily!'
'Parrot hath not dined of all this long day,'
'Like our puss cat Parrot can mew and cry.'
In Latin, in Hebrew, and in Caldee,
In Greek tongue Parrot can both speak and say,
As Percius, that poet, doth report of me,
Quis expeduit psitaco suum Chyre?

Dowche French of Paris Parrot can learn,
Pronouncing my purpose after my property,   30
With, *'Parlez bien, Parrot, ou parlez rien.'*
With Dowche, with Spanish, my tongue can agree;
In English to God Parrot can supply:
'Christ save King Henry the VIIIth, our royal king,
The red rose in honour to flourish and spring!'

'With Katherine incomporable, our royal queen also,
That peerless pomegranate, Christ save her noble grace!'
Parrot *saves habeler Castylyano,*
With *fidasso de cosso* in Turkey and in Thrace;
Vis consilii expers, as teacheth me Horace,   40
Mole ruit sua, whose dictes are pregnant –
'*Soventez foyz,* Parrot, *en sovenaunte.'*

My lady mistress, Dame Philology,
Gave me a gift in my nest when I lay,
To learn all language and it to speak aptly.
Now *pandes mory,* wax frantic some men say;
Phronesis for frenzies may not hold her way.

An almond now for Parrot, delicately dressed;
In *Salve festa dyes, toto* is the best.

Moderata juvant but *toto* doth exceed;   50
Discretion is mother of noble virtues all;
Myden agan in Greek tongue we read,
But reason and wit wanteth their provincial,
When wilfulness is vicar general.
'*Hec res acu tangitur*, Parrot, *par ma foye* – '
'*Tycez-vous*, Parrot, *tenes-vous coye*.'

Busy, busy, busy, and business again!
'*Que pensez-voz*, Parrot? What meaneth this business?'
Vitulus in Oreb troubled Aaron's brain;
Melchisedeck merciful made Moloch merciless.   60
Too wise is no virtue, too medling, too restless;
In measure is treasure, *cum sensu maturato*:
Ne tropo sanno, ne tropo mato.

Aram was fired with Chaldee's fire called Ur;
Jobab was brought up in the land of Hus;
The lineage of Lot took support of Assur;
Jereboseth is Hebrew, who list the cause discuss.
'Peace, Parrot, ye prate as ye were *ebrius!*'
Howst thee, *lyver god ven hemrick, ic seg*;
In Popering grew pears, when Parrot was an egg.   70

'What is this to purpose?' Over in a whinnymeg!
Hop Lobin of Lowdeon would have a bit of bread;
The gibbet of Baldock was made for Jack Leg;
An arrow unfeathered and without an head,
A bagpipe without blowing standeth in no stead:
Some run too far before, some run too far behind,
Some be too churlish, and some be too kind.

Ic dien serveth for the ostrich feather,
Ic dien is the language of the land of Beme;
In Affric tongue *byrsa* is a thong of leather;   80
In Palestine there is Jerusalem.
Collustrum now for Parrot, white bread and sweet cream!
Our Thomasen she doth trip, our Janet she doth shail;
Parrot hath a black beard and a fair green tail.

'Morrish mine own shelf,' the costermonger sayeth;
'Fate, fate, fate, ye Irish water-lag.'
In flattering fables men find but little faith;
But *moveatur terra*, let the world wag,
Let Sir Wrig-wrag wrestle with Sir Delarag:
Every man after his manner of ways,   90
Pawbe une arver, so the Welsh man says.

Such shreads of sentence, stowed in the shop
Of ancient Aristippus and such other mo[re],
I gather together and close in my crop,
Of my wanton conceit, *unde depromo*
Dilemata docta in pedagogio
Sacro vatum, whereof to you I break;
I pray you, let Parrot have liberty to speak.

'But ware the cat, Parrot, ware the false cat!'
With, 'Who is there? A maid?' Nay, nay, I trow!   100
Ware, riot, Parrot, ware riot, ware that!
'Mete, mete, for Parrot, mete I say, how!'
Thus divers of language by learning I grow:
With, 'Bas me, sweet Parrot, bas me, sweet sweet;'
To dwell among ladies, Parrot, is meet.

'Parrot, Parrot, Parrot, pretty popigay!'
With my beak I can pick my little pretty toe;
My delight is solace, pleasure, disport and play;
Like a wanton, when I will, I reel to and fro.
Parrot can say, '*Cesar, ave*', also;   110
But Parrot hath no favour to Esebon;
Above all other birds, set Parrot alone.

Ulula, Esebon, for Jeremy doth weep!
Sion is in sadness, Rachel ruly doth look;
Madionita Jetro, our Moses keepeth his sheep;
Gideon is gone, that Zalmane undertook,
Oreb *et* Zeb, of *Judicum* read the book.
Now Geball, Amon and Amaloch – Hark, hark,
Parrot pretendeth to be a Bible clerk!

O Esebon, Esebon, to thee is come again 120
Seon, the regent *Amorreorum*,
And Og, that fat hog of Basan, doth retain
The crafty *coistronus Cananeorum*;
And *assilum*, whilom *refugium miserorum*,
Non phanum, sed prophanum, standeth in little stead:
Ulula, Esebon, for Jepte is stark dead!

Esebon, Marybon, Weston next Barnet;
A trim-tram for an horse-mill it were a nice thing,
Dainties for dammosels, chaffer far-fet;
Bo-ho doth bark well, Hough-ho he ruleth the ring; 130
From Scarpary to Tartary renoun therein doth spring,
With, 'He said', and 'We said'. Ich wot now what ich wot,
Quod magnus est dominus Judas Scarioth.

Ptolemy and Haley were cunning and wise
In the volvell, in the quadrant and in the astrolabe,
To prognosticate truly the chance of fortune's dice;
Some treat of their theories, some of astrology,
Some *pseudo-propheta* with ciromancy:
If fortune be friendly, and grace be the guide,
Honour with renown will run on the side. 140

    '*Monon Calon Agaton*,' 140a
    Quod Parato
    In Greco.

Let Parrot, I pray you, have liberty to prate,
For *aurea lyngua Greca* ought to be magnified,
If it were conned perfectly, and after the rate,
As *lyngua Latina*, in school matter occupied;
But our Greeks their Greek so well have applied,
That they cannot say in Greek, riding by the way,
'How, ostler, fetch my horse a botell of hay!'

Neither frame a syllogism in *phrisesomorum*
Formaliter et Grece, cum medio termino:
Our Greeks ye wallow in the wash-bowl *Argolicorum*; 150
For though ye can tell in Greek what is *phormio*,

Yet ye seek out your Greek in *Capricornio*;
For ye scrape out good scripture, and set in a gall:
Ye go about to amend, and ye mar all.

Some argue *secundum quid ad simpliciter*,
And yet he would be reckoned *pro Ariopagita*;
And some make distinctions *multipliciter*,
Whether *ita* were before *non*, or *non* before *ita*,
Neither wise nor well learned, but like *hermaphradita*:
Set *Sophia* aside, for every Jack Raker   160
And every mad meddler must now be a maker.

In *Achademia* Parrot dare no problem keep,
For *Greci fari* so occupieth the chair,
That *Latinum fari* may fall to rest and sleep,
And *silogisari* was drowned at Stourbridge Fair;
Trivials and Quatrivials so sore now they appear,
That Parrot the popagay hath pity to behold
How the rest of good learning is ruffled up and trold.

Albertus *De modo significandi*
And Donatus be driven out of school;   170
Prisian's head broken now, handy-dandy,
And *Inter didascolos* is reckoned for a fool;
Alexander, a gander of Menander's pole,
With, '*Da causales*', is cast out of the gate,
And '*Da racionales*' dare not show his pate.

Plautus in his comedies a child shall now rehearse,
And meddle with Quintilian in his *Declamacions*,
That *Petty Caton* can scantly construe a verse,
With, '*Aveto*' in *Greco*, and such solemn salutations,
Can scantly the tenses of his conjugations;   180
Setting their minds so much of eloquence,
That of their school matters lost is the whole sentence.

Now a nutmeg, a nutmeg, *cum gariopholo*,
For Parrot to pick upon, his brain for to stable,
Sweet cinnamon sticks and *pleris cum musco*!
In Paradise, that place of pleasure perdurable,

The progeny of Parrots were fair and favorable;
Now *in valle* Ebron Parrot is fain to feed:
'Christ's cross and Saint Nicholas, Parrot, be your good speed!'

The mirror that I tote in, *quasi diaphonum*,   190
Vel quasi speculum, in enigmate,
Elencticum, or else *enthimematicum*,
For logicians to look on, somewhat *sophistice*;
Rhetoricians and orators in fresh humanity,
Support Parrot, I pray you, with your sufferage ornate,
Of *confuse tantum* avoiding the checkmate.

But of that supposition that called is art,
Confuse distrybutyve, as Parrot hath devised,
Let every man after his merit take his part;
For in this process, Parrot nothing hath surmised,   200
No matter pretended, nor nothing enterprised,
But that *metaphora, alegoria* withall,
Shall be his protection, his pavis and his wall.

For Parrot is no churlish chough, nor no flecked [mag]pie,
Parrot is no pendugum, that men call a carling,
Parrot is no woodcock, nor no butterfly,
Parrot is no stammering stare, that men call a starling;
But Parrot is my own dear heart, and my dear darling.
Melpomene, that fair maid, she burnished his beak:
I pray you, let Parrot have liberty to speak.   210

Parrot is a fair bird for a lady;
God of his goodness him framed and wrought;
When Parrot is dead, he doth not putrify;
Ye, all thing mortal shall turn unto nought
Except man's soul, that Christ so dear bought;
That never may die, nor never die shall:
Make much of Parrot, the popagay royal.

For that peerless prince that Parrot did create,
He made you of nothing by his majesty;
Point well this problem that Parrot doth prate,   220
And remember among how Parrot and ye

Shall leap from this life, as merry as we be.
Pomp, pride, honour, riches and worldly lust,
Parrot sayeth plainly, shall turn all to dust.

Thus Parrot doth pray you,
With heart most tender,
To reckon with this recule now
And it to remember.

Psitacius, ecce, cano, nec sunt mea carmina Phebo
Digna scio, tamen est plena camena deo.   230

Secondum Skeltonida famigeratum,
In Piereorum cathalogo numeratum.

Itaque consolamyni invicem in verbis istis, etc.   232a
Candidi lectores, callide callete, vestrum fovete Psitacum, etc.

GALATHEA
Speak, Parrot, I pray you, for Mary's sake,   232c
What moan he made when Pamphilus lost his mate.

PARROT
My proper Besse,
My pretty Besse,
Turn once again to me;
For sleepest thou, Besse,
Or wakest thou, Besse,
Mine heart it is with thee.   240

My daisy delectable,
My primrose commendable,
My violet amiable,
My joy inexplicable,
Now turn again to me.

I will be firm and stable,
And to you serviceable,
And also profitable,
If ye be agreeable,

My proper Besse,   250
To turn again to me.

Alas, I am disdained,
And as a man half-maimed,
My heart is so sore pained,
I pray thee, Besse, unfeigned,
Yet come again to me!

By love I am constrained
To be with you retained,
It will not be refrained:
I pray you be reclaimed,   260
My proper Besse,
And turn again to me!

Quod Parrot, thy popagay royal. [. . .]

Lenvoy primere
Go, little quire, named the Popagay,
Home to resort Jerobesethe persuade;
For the cliffs of Scaloppe they roar weilaway,   280
And the sands of Cefas begin to waste and fade,
For replication restless that he of late there made;
Now Neptune and Aeolus are agreed of likelihood,
For Titus at Dover abideth in the road;

Lucina she wadeth among the watery floods,
And the cocks begin to crow against the day;
Le tonsan de Jason is lodged among the shrouds;
Of Argus revenged, recover when he may,
Lycaon of Libya and Lydia hath caught his prey:
Go, little quire, pray them that you behold,   290
In their remembrance ye may be enrolled.

Yet some fools say ye are furnished with knacks,
That hang together as feathers in the wind;
But lewdly are they lettered that your learning lacks,
Barking and whining like churlish curs of kind,
For who looketh wisely in your works may find

Much fruitful matter. But now for your defence,
Again all remords arm you with patience. [. . .]

Secunde Lenvoy

Pass forth, Parrot, towards some passenger;
Require him to convey you over the salt foam;
Addressing yourself, like a sad messenger,
To our sullen seigneur Sadoke, desire him to come home,
Making his pilgrimage by *Nostre Dame de Crome*:
For Jerico and Jersey shall meet together as soon
As he to exploit the man out of the moon.

With porpoise and grandepose he may feed him fat,
Though he pamper not his paunch with the great seal;
We have longed and looked long time for that,   310
Which causeth poor suitors have many a hungry meal;
As president and regent he ruleth every deal.
Now pass forth, good Parrot, Our Lord be your stead,
In this your journey to prosper and speed.

And though some disdain you and say how ye prate,
And how your poems are barren of polished eloquence,
There is none that your name will abbrogate
Than noddypolls and grammatols of small intelligence:
Too rude is their reason to reach to your sentence;
Such melancholy mastiffs and mangy cur dogs   320
Are meet for a swine-herd to hunt after hogs.

Monosticon

Psitace, perge volans, fatuorum tela retundas.   322b
Merda! puros mall desers!
In diebus Novembris

Le dereyn lenvoy

Prepare you, Parrot, bravely your passage to take,
Of Mercury under the triurnal aspect,
And sadly salute our sullen Sir Sydrake,
And show him that all the world doth conject,

How the matters he meddles in come to small effect;
For he wanteth of his wits that all would rule alone;
It is no little burden to bear a great mill stone. 330

To bring all the sea into a cherrystone-pit,
To number all the stars in the firmament,
To rule nine realms by one man's wit,
To such things impossible, reason cannot consent;
Much money, men say, there madly he hath spent;
Parrot, ye may prate this under protestation,
Was never such a senator since Christ's Incarnation.

Wherfore he may now come again as he went,
Non sine postica sanna, as I trow,
From Calais to Dover, to Canterbury in Kent, 340
To make reckoning in the receipt how Robin lost his bow,
To sow corn in the sea-sand, there will no crop grow,
Though ye be taunted, Parrot, with tongues attainted,
Yet your problems are pregnant and with loyalty acquainted.

Monasticon
I, properans, Parrot, malas sic coripe linguas.
Merda! puros mall desires!
15 Kalendis Decembris

Dysticon miserabill

Altior, heu, cedro, crudelior, heu, leopardo;
Heu, vitulus bubali fit dominus Priami!

Tetrasticon
Non annis licet et Priamus sed honore voceris:
Dum foveas vitulum, res, regeris, Britonum; 350
Rex, regeris, non ipse regis, rex inclite, calle;
Subde tibi vitulum ne fatuet nimium.

God amend all,

That all amend may!
Amen, quod Parrot,
the royal popagay.

Kalendis Decembris

Lenvoy royall

Go, proper Parrot, my popagay,
That lordes and ladies this pamphlet may behold,
With notable clerks; supply to them, I pray,
Your rudeness to pardon and also that they would   360
Vouchsafe to defend you against the brawling scold
Called Detraction, encankered with envy,
Whose tongue is attainted with slanderous obliqui.

For truth in parable ye wantonly pronounce,
Languages diverse; yet under that doth rest
Matters more precious than the rich jacounce,
Diamond, or ruby, or balas of the best,
Of Inde sapphire with orient pearls dressed:
Wherefore your remorders are mad or else stark blind,
You to remord erst or they know your mind.   370

Disticon
I, volitans, Parrotte tuam moderare Minervam:
Vix tua percipient, qui tua teque legent.

Hyperbaton
Psitacus heu notus seu Percius est, puto, notus,
Nec, reor, est nec erit, licet est erit undique notus.
Maledite soyte bouche malheurewse!

Laucture de Parrot

O My Parrot, O unice dilecte, votorum meorum
Omnis lapis, lapis preciosus operimentum tuum!

PARROT
Sicut Aron populumque,

Sic bubali vitulus,
Sic bubali vitulus,
Sic bubali vitulus. 380

Thus much Parrot hath openly expressed;
Let's see who dare make up the rest.

Le Popagay sen va complayndre 382a

Helas! I lament the dull abused brain,
The infatuate fantasies, the witless wilfulness
Of one and other at me that have disdain.
Some say they cannot my parables express;
Some say I rail at riot reckless;
Some say but little and think more in their thought,
How this process I prate of, it is not all for nought.

O causeless cowards, O heartless hardiness, 390
O manless manhood, enfainted all with fear,
O cunning clergy, where is your readiness
To practise or postell this process here and there?
For dread ye dare not meddle with such gear,
Or else ye pinch courtesy, truly as I trow,
Which of you first dare boldly pluck the crow?

The sky is cloudy, the coast is nothing clear;
Titon hath trussed up his tresses of fine gold;
Jupiter for Saturn dare make no royal cheer;
Lycaon laugheth thereat and beareth him more bold; 400
Rachel, ruefully ragged, she is like to catch cold;
Moloch, that mawmett, there dare no man withsay;
The rest of such reckoning may make a foul fray.

Dixit, quod Parrot, the royal popagay.

PARROT
Jupiter ut nitido deus est veneratus Olimpo;
Hic coliturque deus.
Sunt data thura Jovi, rutilo solio residenti;
Cum Jove thura capit.

Jupiter astrorum rector dominusque polorum;
Anglica sceptra refit.   410

GALATHEA
I compass the conveyance unto the capital
Of our clerk Cleros. Whither, thidder and why not hither?
For pass-a-Pase apase is gone to catch a mole,
Over Scarpary *mala vy*, Monsieur Cy-and-slidder.
What sequel shall follow when pendugims meet together?
Speak, Parrot, my sweet bird, and ye shall have a date,
Of franticness and foolishness which is the greatest state?

PARROT
Difficult it is to answer this demand;
Yet, after the sagacity of a popagay,
Franticness doth rule and all thing command;   420
Wilfulness and Brainless now rule all the ray.
Against Frantic Frenzy there dare no man say nay,
For Franticness and Wilfulness and Brainless *ensemble*,
The nebbis of a lion they make to treat and tremble,

To jumble, to stumble, to tumble down like fools;
To lower, to droop, to kneel, to stoop and to play couch-quail;
To fish afore the net and to draw poles.
He maketh them to bear baubles, and to bear a low sail;
He carrieth a king in his sleeve, if all the world fail;
He faceth out at a flush with, 'Show, take all!'   430
Of Pope Julius's cards, he is chief card-in-all.

He triumpheth, he trumpeth, he turneth all up and down,
With, 'Skyre-galiard, proud paliard, vaunt-parler, ye prate!'
His wolf's head, wan, blue as lead, gapeth over the crown;
It is to fear lest he would wear the garland on his pate,
Par-equal with all princes, far passing his estate;
For of our regent the regiment he hath, *ex qua vi*,
Patet per versus quod ex vi bolte harvi.

Now, Galathea, let Parrot, I pray you, have his date –
Yet dates now are dainty, and wax very scanty,   440
For grocers were grudged at and groaned at but late;

Great reasons with raisins be now reprobitant,
For raisins are no reasons but reasons currant –
Run God, run Devil! Yet the date of Our Lord
And the date of the Devil doth shrewdly accord.

Dixit, quod Parrot, the popagay royal.

GALATHEA
Now, Parrot, my sweet bird, speak out yet once again,
Set aside all sophisms, and speak now true and plain.

PARROT
So many moral matters, and so little used;
So much new making, and so mad time spent;   450
So much translation into English confused;
So much noble preaching, and so little amendment;
So much consultation, almost to none intent;
So much provision, and so little wit at need –
Since Deucalion's flood there can no clerks read.

So little discretion, and so much reasoning;
So much hardy-dardy, and so little manliness;
So prodigal expense, and so shameful reckoning;
So gorgeous garments, and so much wretchedness,
So much portly pride, with purses penniless;   460
So much spent before, and so much unpaid behind –
Since Deucalion's flood there can no clerks find.

So much forecasting, and so far an after-deal;
So much politic prating, and so little standeth in stead;
So little secretness, and so much great counsel;
So many bold barons, their hearts as dull as lead;
So many noble bodies, under one daw's head;
So royal a king, as reigneth upon us all –
Since Deucalion's flood, was never seen nor shall.

So many complaints, and so small redress;   470
So much calling on, and so small taking heed;
So much loss of merchandise, and so remediless;
So little care for the commonweal, and so much need;

So much doubtful danger, and so little dread;
So much pride of prelates, so cruel and so keen –
Since Deucalion's flood, I trow, was never seen.

So many thieves hanged, and thieves nevertheless;
So much imprisonment, for matters not worth a hawe;
So much papers wearing for right a small excess;
So much pillory pageants under colour of good law;   480
So much turning on the cook-stole for every guy-gaw;
So much mockish making of statutes of array –
Since Deucalion's flood was never, I dare say.

So brainless calves' heads, so many sheep's tails;
So bold a bragging butcher, and flesh sold so dear;
So many plucked partridges, and so fat quails;
So mangy a mastiff cur, the great greyhound's peer;
So big a bulk of brow-antlers cabbaged that year;
So many swans dead, and so small revel –
Since Deucalion's flood, I trow, no man can tell.   490

So many truces taken, and so little perfect trowth;
So muche belly-joy, and so wasteful banqueting;
So pinching and sparing, and so little profit groweth,
So many huge houses building, and so small house-holding;
Such statutes upon diets, such pilling and polling –
So is all thing wrought wilfully without reason and skill.
Since Deucalion's flood the world was never so ill.

So many vagabonds, so many beggars bold,
So much decay of monasteries and religious places;
So hot hatred against the Church, and charity so cold;   500
So much of 'my lord's grace', and in him no grace is;
So many hollow hearts, and so double faces;
So much sanctuary breaking, and privilege barred –
Since Deucalion's flood was never seen nor heard.

So much ragged right of a ram's horn;
So rigorous revelling, in a prelate specially;
So bold and so bragging, and was so basely born;
So lordly of his looks, and so disdainously;

So fat a maggot, bred of a flesh-fly;
Was never such a filthy gorgon, nor such an epicure,   510
Since Deucalion's flood, I make thee fast and sure.

So much privy watching in cold winter's nights;
So much searching of losells, and is himself so lewd;
So much conjurations for elvish midday sprites;
So many bulls of pardon published and showed;
So much crossing and blessing and him all beshrewed;
Such pole-axes and pillers, such mules trapped with gold –
Since Deucalion's flood, in no chronicle is told.

    Dixit, quod Parrot

Crescet in immensem me vivo Psitacus iste;
Hinc mea dicetur Skeltonidis inclita fama.   520
       Quod Skelton Laureate
        Orator Regius

Colin Cloute

Hereafter followeth a little book called Colin Cloute,
compiled by Master Skelton, poet laureate

Quis consurget mecum adversus malignantes?
aut quis stabit mecum adversus operantes
iniquitatem? Nemo, Domine!

      What can it avail
      To drive forth a snail,
      Or to make a sail
      Of an herring's tail;
      To rhyme or to rail,
      To write or to indict,
      Either for delight
      Or else for despite;

Or books to compile
Of divers manner style,   10
Vice to revile
And sin to exile;
To teach or to preach,
As reason will reach?
Say this, and say that,
His head is so fat,
He wotteth never what
Nor whereof he speaketh;
He cryeth and he creaketh,
He pryeth and he peeketh,   20
He chides and he chatters,
He prates and he patters,
He clitters and he clatters,
He meddles and he smatters,
He gloses and he flatters;
Or, if he speak plain,
Then he lacketh brain,
He is but a fool;
Let him go to school,
On a three-footed stool   30
That he may down sit,
For he lacketh wit;
And if that he hit
The nail on the head,
It standeth in no stead;
The devil, they say, is dead,
The devil is dead.

It may well so be,
Or else they would see
Otherwise, and flee   40
From worldly vanity,
And foul covetousness,
And other wretchedness,
Fickle falseness,
Variableness,
With unstableness.

And if ye stand in doubt
Who brought this rhyme about,

My name is Colin Cloute.
I purpose to shake out   50
All my cunning bag,
Like a clerkly hag;
For though my rhyme be ragged,
Tattered and jagged,
Rudely rain beaten,
Rusty and moth-eaten,
If ye take well therewith,
It hath in it some pith.
For, as far as I can see,
It is wrong with each degree: 60
For the temporality
Accuseth the spirituality;
The spiritual again
Doth grudge and complain
Upon the temporal men:
Thus each of other blother
The one against the other:
Alas, they make me shudder!
For in hugger-mugger
The Church is put in fault;   70
The prelates be so haught,
They say, and look so high,
As though they would fly
Above the starry sky.
   Lay men say indeed
How they take no heed
Their silly sheep to feed,
But pluck away and pull
The fleeces of their wool,
Unneth they leave a lock   80
Of wool among their flock;
And as for their cunning,
A glomming and a mumming,
And make thereof a jape;
They gasp and they gape
All to have promotion,
There is their whole devotion,
With money, if it will hap,

To catch the forked cap:
Forsooth they are too lewd   90
To say so, all beshrewed!
   What trow ye they say more
Of the bishop's lore?
How in matters they be raw,
They lumber forth the law,
To hearken Jack and Jill,
When they put up a bill,
And judge it as they will,
For other men's skill,
Expounding out their clauses,   100
And leave their own causes:
In their provincial cure
They make but little sure,
And meddle very light
In the Church's right;
But *ire* and *venire*,
And solfa '*so ala mire*',
That the *praemunire*
Is like to be set afire
In their jurisdictions   110
Through temporal afflictions:
Men say they have prescriptions,
Against spiritual contradictions,
Accounting them as fictions.
   And whilst the heads do this,
The remnant is amiss
Of the clergy all,
Both great and small.
I woot never how they work,
But thus the people bark;   120
And surely thus they say,
Bishops, if they may,
Small houses would keep,
But slumber forth and sleep,
And assay to creep
Within the noble walls
Of the king's halls,
To fat their bodies full,

Their souls lean and dull,
And have full little care   130
How evil their sheep fare. [. . .]
    Thus I, Colin Cloute,
As I go about,
And wandering as I walk,
I hear the people talk.   290
Men say, for silver and gold
Mitres are bought and sold;
There shall no clergy oppose
A mitre nor a crosier,
But a full purse:
A straw for God's curse!
What are they the worse?
For a Simoniac
Is but a Hermoniac;
And no more ye make   300
Of simony, men say,
But a child's play.
    Over this, the foresaid lay
Report how the Pope may
An holy anchor call
Out of the stony wall,
And him a bishop make,
If he on him dare take
To keep so hard a rule,
To ride upon a mule   310
With gold all betrapped,
In purple and paul belapped;
Some hatted and some capped,
Richly bewrapped,
God woot to their great pains,
In rotchettes of fine Rennes,
White as mare's milk;
Their tabards of fine silk,
Their stirrups of mixed gold beggared;
There may no cost be spared;   320
Their mules gold doth eat,
Their neighbours die for meat.
    What care they though Jill sweat,

Or Jack of the Noke?
The poor people they yoke
With summons and citations
And excommunications,
About churches and market:
The bishop on his carpet
At home full soft doth sit.   330
This is a fairly fit,
To hear the people jangle,
How warely they wrangle:
Alas, why do ye not handle
And them all to-mangle?
Full falsely on you they lie,
And shamefully you ascrie,
And say as untruly,
As the butterfly
A man might say in mock   340
Ware the weathercock
Of the steeple of Paul's;
And thus they hurt their souls
In slandering you for truth:
Alas, it is great ruth!
Some say ye sit in thrones,
Like princes *aquilonis*,
And shrine your rotten bones
With pearls and precious stones;
But how the commons groans,   350
And the people moans
For prests and for loans
Lent and never paid,
But from day to day delayed,
The common wealth decayed,
Men say ye are tongue-tied,
And thereof speak nothing
But dissimuling and glosing.
Wherfore men be supposing
That ye give shrewd counsel   360
Against the commonweal,
By polling and pillage
In cities and village,

By taxing and tollage,
Ye make monks to have the culerage
For covering of an old cottage,
That committed is a collage
In the charter of dotage,
Tenure par servyce de sottage,
And not *par servyce de socage,*   370
After old seigneurs,
And the learning of Littleton's *Tenures:*
Ye have so overthwarted,
That good laws are subverted,
And good reason perverted.
   Religious men are fain
For to turn again
In secula seculorum,
And to forsake their corum,
And *vagabundare per forum,*   380
And take a fine *meritorum,*
Contra regulam morum,
Aut black *monachorum,*
Aut canonicorum,
Aut Bernardinorum,
Aut crucifixorum,
And to sing from place to place,
Like apostates.
   And the self-same game
Begun is now with shame   390
Amongst the sely nuns:
My lady now she runs,
Dame Sibil our abbess,
Dame Dorothy and lady Besse
Dame Sara our prioress,
Out of their cloister and choir
With an heavy cheer,
Must cast up their black veils,
And set up their fuck sails,
To catch wind with their ventales –   400
What, Colin, there thou shales!
Yet thus with ill hails
The lay fee people rails.

And all the fault they lay
On you, prelates, and say
Ye do them wrong and no right
To put them thus to flight;
No matins at midnight,
Book and chalice gone quite;
And pluck away the leads 410
Even over their heads,
And sell away their bells,
And all that they have else:
Thus the people tells,
Rails like rebels,
Reads shrewdly and spells,
And with foundations mells,
And talks like titivelles,
How ye break the dead's wills,
Turn monasteries into water-mills, 420
Of an abbey ye make a grange;
Your works, they say, are strange;
So that their founders' souls
Have lost their bead-rolls,
The money for their masses
Spent among wanton lasses;
The *Diriges* are forgotten;
Their founders lie there rotten,
But where their souls dwell,
Therewith I will not mell. 430
What could the Turk do more
With all his false lore,
Turk, Saracen, or Jew?
I report me to you,
O merciful Jesu,
You support and rescue,
My style for to direct,
It may take some effect!
For I abhor to write
How the lay fee despite 440
You prelates, that of right
Should be lanterns of light.
Ye live, they say, in delight,

Drowned *in deliciis,*
In gloria et divitiis,
In admirabili honore,
In gloria, et splendore
Fulgurantis hastæ,
Viventes parum caste:
Yet sweet meat hath sour sauce,   450
For after *gloria, laus,*
Christ by cruelty
Was nailed upon a tree;
He paid a bitter pension
For man's redemption,
He drank eisell and gall
To redeem us withall;
But sweet hippocras ye drink,
With, 'Let the cat wink!'
Ich woot what ich do think;   460
How be it *per assimile*
Some men think that ye
Shall have penalty
For your iniquity.
Nota what I say,
And bear it well away;
If it please not theology,
It is good astrology;
For Ptolemy told me
The sun sometime to be   470
In Ariete,
Ascendent a degree,
When Scorpion descending,
Was so then pretending
A fatal fall of one
That should sit on a throne,
And rule all things alone.
Your teeth whet on this bone
Amongst you everyone,
And let Colin Cloute have none   480
Manner of cause to moan:
Lay salve to your own sore,
For else, as I said before,

After *gloria, laus,*
May come a sour sauce;
Sorry therfore am I,
But truth can never lie. [. . .]
Ye bishops of estates
Should open the broad gates
Of your spiritual charge,
And come forth at large,
Like lanterns of light,
In the people's sight,
In pulpits authentic,
For the weal public
Of priesthood in this case;   700
And always to chase
Such manner of schismatics
And half heretics,
That would intoxicate,
That would conquinate,
That would contaminate,
And that would violate,
And that would derogate,
And that would abrogate
The Church's high estates,   710
After this manner rates,
The which should be
Both frank and free,
And have their liberty,
As of antiquity
It was ratified,
And also gratified,
By holy synodals
And bulls papals,
As it is *res certa*   720
Contained in *Magna Carta.* [. . .]
   But now my mind ye understand,
For they must take in hand   890
To preach, and to withstand
All manner of abjections;
For bishops have protections,
They say, to do corrections,

But they have no affections
To take the said directions;
In such manner of cases,
Men say, they bear no faces
To occupy such places,
To sow the seed of graces: 900
Their hearts are so fainted,
And they be so attainted
With covetice and ambition,
And other superstition,
That they be deaf and dumb,
And play silence and glum,
Can say nothing but 'mum'.
    They occupy them so
With singing *Placebo*,
They will no farther go: 910
They had lever to please,
And take their worldly ease,
Than to take on hand
Worshipfully to withstand
Such temporal war and bate,
As now is made of late
Against holy Church's estate,
Or to maintain good quarels.
The lay men call them barrels
Full of gluttony   920
And of hyprocrisy,
That counterfeits and paints
As they were very saints:
In matters that them like
They show them politic,
Pretending gravity
And seniority,
With all solemnity,
For their indemnity;
For they will have no loss   930
Of a penny nor of a cross
Of their predial lands,
That cometh to their hands,
And as far as they dare set,

All is fish that cometh to net:
Building royally
Their mansions curiously,
With turrets and with towers,
With halls and with bowers,
Stretching to the stars,   940
With glass windows and bars;
Hanging about the walls
Cloths of gold and pauls,
Arras of rich array,
Fresh as flowers in May;
With Dame Diana naked;
How lusty Venus quaked,
And how Cupid shaked
His dart, and bent his bow
For to shoot a crow   950
At her tirly tirlow;
And how Paris of Troy
Danced a *lege de moy*,
Made lusty sport and joy
With Dame Helen the queen;
With such stories between
Their chambers well beseen;
With triumphs of Caesar,
And of Pompey's war,
Of renown and of fame   960
By them to get a name:
Now all the world stares,
How they ride in goodly chairs,
Conveyed by elephants,
With laureate garlands,
And by unicorns
With their seemly horns;
Upon these beasts riding,
Naked boys striding,
With wanton wenches winking.   970
Now truly, to my thinking,
That is a speculation
And a meet meditation
For prelates of estate,

Their courage to abate
From worldly wantonness,
Their chambers thus to dress
With such perfectness
And all such holiness;
How be it they let down fall 980
Their churches cathedral.
    Squire, knight, and lord,
Thus the Church remord;
With all temporal people
They run against the steeple
Thus talking and telling
How some of you are meddling;
Yet soft and fair for swelling,
Beware of a queen's yelling.
It is a busy thing 990
For one man to rule a king
Alone and make reckoning,
To govern over all
And rule a realm royal
By one man's very wit;
Fortune may chance to flit,
And when he weneth to sit,
Yet may he miss the cushion:
For I read a proposition
Cum regibus amicare, 1000
Et omnibus dominari,
Et supra te pravare;
Wherefore he hath good ure
That can himself assure
How fortune will endure.
Then let reason you support,
For the communalty doth report
That they have great wonder
That ye keep them so under;
Yet they marvel so much less, 1010
For ye play so at the chess,
As they suppose and guess,
That some of you but late
Hath played so checkmate

With lords of great estate,
After such a rate,
That they shall mell nor make,
Nor upon them take,
For king nor kaiser's sake,
But at the pleasure of one   1020
That ruleth the roost alone. [. . .]

Why Come Ye Not to Court?

All noble men of this take heed,
And believe it as your creed.

Too hasty of sentence,
Too fierce for none offence,
Too scarce of your expense,
Too large in negligence,
Too slack in recompense,
Too haught in excellence,
Too light intelligence,
And too light in credence;   10
Where these keep residence,
Reason is banished thence,
And also Dame Prudence,
With sober Sapience.

All noble men of this take heed,
And believe it as your creed.

Then, without collusion,
Mark well this conclusion:
Through such abusion,
And by such illusion,   20
Unto great confusion
A noble man may fall,
And his honour appal.
And if ye think this shall

Not rub you on the gall,
Then the devil take all!

All noble men of this take heed,
And believe it as your creed.

Hec vates ille
De quo loquntur mille.   30

   Why come ye not to court?

For age is a page
For the court full unmeet;
For age cannot rage,
Nor bass her sweet sweet.
   But when age seeth that rage
Doth assuage and refrain,
Then will age have a courage
To come to court again.

But   40
Helas! sage overage
So madly decays,
That age for dotage
Is reckoned nowadays.
   Thus age, (a *graunt domage*),
Is nothing set by,
And rage in arrearage
Doth run lamentably.

So
That rage must make pillage   50
To catch that catch may,
And with such forage
Hunt the boskage,
That harts will run away,
Both harts and hinds
With all good minds.
Farewell, then, have good day! [. . .]

Dicken, thou crow doubtless!
For truly to express,
There hath been much excess: 70
With banqueting brainless,
With rioting reckless,
With gambling thriftless,
With, 'Spend', and waste witless,
Treating of truce restless,
Prating for peace peaceless.
The countering at Cales
Wrang us on the males!
Chief counsellor was careless,
Groaning, grouching, graceless,   80
And to none intent,
Our tall-wood is all brent,
Our faggots are all spent.
We may blow at the coal!
Our mare hath cast her foal,
And, 'Mocke hath lost her shoe;
What may she do thereto?'
An end of an old song:
'Do right and do no wrong.'
As right as a ram's horn!   90
For thrift is threadbare worn,
Our sheep are shrewdly shorn,
And truth is all too-torn;
Wisdom is laughed to scorn,
Favell is false forsworn,
Javell is nobly born;
Havell and Harvy Hafter,
Jack Travell and Cole Crafter,
We shall hear more hereafter!
With polling and shaving,   100
With borrowing and craving,
With reaving and raving,
With swearing and staring,
There availeth no reasoning;
For Will doth rule all thing,
Will, Will, Will, Will, Will!
He ruleth always still.
Good Reason and good Skill,

They may garlic peel,
Carry sacks to the mill,   110
Of peascods they may shell,
Or else go roast a stone!
There is no man but one
That hath the strokes alone;
Be it black or white
All that he doth is right,
As right as a cammock crooked!
This bill well overlooked,
Clearely perceive we may
There went the hare away;   120
The hare, the fox, the gray,
The hart, the hind, the buck.
God send us better luck!
God send us better luck, etc.

Twit, Andrew! Twit, Scot!
Ge heme! ge scour thy pot,
For we have spent our shot!
We shall have a *tot quot*
From the Pope of Rome
To weave all in one loom   130
A web of lisle-wulsey,
Opus male dulce!
The devil kiss his cule!
For whiles he doth rule,
All is worse and worse.
The devil kiss his arse!
For whether he bless or curse,
It cannot be much worse.
From Bamborough to Bootham Bar
We have cast up our war,   140
And made a worthy truce.
With, 'Gup, levell suse!'
Our money madly lent,
And more madly spent.
From Croydon into Kent
Woote ye whither they went?
From Winchelsea to Rye

And all not worth a fly,
From Wentbridge to Hull,
Our army waxeth dull,   150
With, 'Turn all home again!'
And never a Scot slain!
Yet the good Earl of Surrey,
The French men he doth fray,
And vexeth them day by day
With all the power he may.
The French men he hath fainted,
And made their hearts attainted.
Of chivalry he is the flower;
Our Lord be his succour!   160
The French men he hath so mated,
And their courage abated,
That they are but half men;
Like foxes in their den,
Like cankered cowards all,
Like urchins in a stone wall,
They keep them in their holds
Like hen-hearted cuckolds.

But yet they over-shoot us
With crowns and with scutus;   170
With scutus and crowns of gold
I dread we are bought and sold.
It is wondrous work.
They shoot all at one mark:
At the Cardinal's hat.
They shoot all at that!
Out of their strong towns
They shoot at him with crowns.
With crowns of gold emblased
They make him so amazed,   180
And his eyes so dazed,
That he ne see can
To know God nor man.
He is set so high
In his hierarchy
Of frantic frenzy

And foolish fantasy,
That in the Chamber of Stars
All matters there he mars,
Clapping his rod on the board.   190
No man dare speak a word,
For he hath all the saying
Without any renaying.
He rolleth in his records,
He sayeth, 'How say ye, my lords?
Is not my reason good?'
Good evening, good Robin Hood!
Some say 'yes', and some
Sit still as they were dumb.
Thus thwarting over them,   200
He ruleth all the roost
With bragging and with boast,
Born up on every side
With pomp and with pride,
With, 'Tromp up!' 'Alleluya!'
For Dame Philargaria
Hath so his heart in hold,
He loveth nothing but gold;
And Asmodeus of Hell
Maketh his members swell   210
With Dalyda to mell,
That wanton damosell. [. . .]

Helas, my heart is sorry
To tell of vainglory;
But now upon this story
I will no further rhyme   230
Till another time;
Till another time, etc.

What news? What news?

Small news that true is
That be worth two kues.
But at the naked Stews
I understand how that

The Sign of the Cardinal's Hat,
That inn, is now shut up,
With, 'Gup, whore, gup! Now gup.   240
Gup, Guilliam Travillian!' [. . .]

What hear ye of the Scots?

They make us all sots,
Popping foolish daws.
They make us to pull straws;
They play their old pranks
After Huntley Banks.
At the stream of Bannockburn
They did us a shrewd turn,
Whan Edward of Caernarvon   270
Lost all his father won.

What hear ye of the lord Dacres?

He maketh us Jack Rakers;
He says we are but crakers;
He calleth us England men
Strong-hearted like an hen.
For the Scots and he,
Too well they do agree,
With, 'Do thou for me,
And I shall do for thee.'   280
Whiles the red hat doth endure,
He maketh himself cocksure.
The red hat with his lure
Bringeth all things under cure.

But as the world now goes,
What hear ye of the lord Roos?

Nothing to purpose
Not worth a cockly fose!
Their hearts be in their hose!
The Earl of Northumberland   290
Dare take nothing on hand.

Our barons be so bold,
Into a mouse-hole they would
Run away and creep;
Like a many of sheep
Dare not look out at door
For dread of the mastiff cur,
For dread of the butcher's dog
Would worry them like an hog.
   For and this cur do gnaw, 300
They must stand all afar
To hold up their hand at the bar.
For all their noble blood,
He plucks them by the hood,
And shakes them by the ear,
And brings them in such fear.
He baiteth them like a bear,
Like an ox or a bull;
Their wits, he sayeth, are dull;
He sayeth they have no brain 310
Their estate to maintain;
And maketh them to bow their knee
Before his majesty.

Judges of the king's laws,
He counts them fools and daws;
Sergeants of the Coif eke,
He sayeth, they are to seek
In pleading of their case
At the Commune Place,
Or at the King's Bench. 320
He wringeth them such a wrench,
That all our learned men
Dare not set their pen
To plead a true trial
Within Westminster Hall.
In the Chancery where he sits
But such as he admits,
None so hardy to speak,
   He sayeth, 'Thou huddy-peke!
Thy learnyng is too lewd, 330

Thy tongue is not well thewed,
To seek before our grace.'
And openly in that place
He rages and he raves,
And calls them cankered knaves.
Thus royally he doth deal
Under the king's broad seal;
And in the Checker he them checks,
In the Star Chamber he nods and becks,
And beareth him there so stout   340
That no man dare rout;
Duke, earl, baron, nor lord,
But to his sentence must accord.
Whether he be knight or squire,
All men must follow his desire. [. . .]

    Yet what hear ye tell
    Of our grand counsel?   380

I could say somewhat,
But speak ye no more of that,
For dread of the red hat
Take pepper in the nose;
For then thine head off goes.
Off by the hard arse!
But there is some traverse
Between some and some
That makes our sire too glum.
It is somewhat wrong   390
That his beard is so long.
He mourneth in black clothing.

I pray God save the king.
Where ever he go or ride
I pray God be his guide.
Thus will I conclude my style,
And fall to rest awhile:
And so to rest a while etc.

Once yet again
Of you I would fain   400
Why come ye not to court?

To which court?
To the king's court?
Or to Hampton Court?

   Nay, to the king's court!
The king's court
Should have the excellence;
But Hampton Court
Hath the pre-eminence!
And York Place,   410
With, 'My lord's grace',
To whose magnificence
Is all the confluence,
Suits and supplications,
Embassies of all nations,
Straw for law canon,
Or for law common,
Or for law civil;
It shall be as he will.
Stop at law Tancred,   420
An abstract or a concrete,
Be it sour, be it sweet!
His wisdom is so discreet
That in a fume or an heat,
'Warden of the Fleet,
Set him fast by the feet!'
And of his royal power
When him list to lower,
Then, 'Have him to the Tower
Saunz aulter remedy!   430
Have him forth by and by
To the Marshalsea,
Or to the King's Bench!'
He diggeth so in the trench
Of the court royal
That he ruleth them all.
So he doth undermine,

And such sleights doth find,
That the king's mind
By him is subverted;   440
And so straightly courted
In credencing his tales,
That all is but nutshells
That any other sayeth,
He hath in him such faith.

Now yet all this might be
Suffered and taken *in gre*
If that that he wrought
To any good end were brought.
But all he bringeth to nought,   450
By God that me dear bought!
   He beareth the king on hand
That he must pill his land
To make his coffers rich;
But he layeth all in the ditch,
And useth such abusion,
That in the conclusion
All commeth to confusion.
Perceive the cause why:
To tell the truth plainly,   460
He is so ambitious,
So shameless and so vicious,
And so superstitious,
And so much oblivious
From whence that he came,
That he falleth into *Acidiam*,
Which, truly to express,
Is a forgetfulness,
Or wilfull blindness,
Wherewith the Sodomites   470
Lost their inward sights.
   The Gomorrans also
Were brought to deadly woe,
As scripture records
A cecitate cordis,
In the Latin sing we,

Lybera nos domine!
   But this mad Amalecke,
Like to a Mamelek,
He regardeth lords   480
No more than potsherds.
He is in such elation
Of his exaltation,
And the supportation
Of our sovereign lord,
That, God to record,
He ruleth all at will
Without reason or skill.
How be it the primordial
Of his wretched original,   490
And his base progeny,
And his greasy genealogy,
He came of the *sang royal*
That was cast out of a butcher's stall!

But, however he was born,
Men would have the less scorn
If he could consider
His birth and room together,
And call to his mind
How noble and how kind   500
To him he hath found
Our sovereign lord, chief ground
Of all this prelacy,
And set him nobly
In great authority
Out from a low degree,
Which he cannot see.
For he was, parde,
No doctor of divinity,
Nor doctor of the law,   510
Nor of none other saw;
But a poor master of art!
God woot, had little part
Of the quatrivials,
Or yet of trivials;

Nor of philosophy,
Nor of philology,
Nor of good policy,
Nor of astronomy;
Nor acquainted worth a fly   520
With honourable Haly,
Nor with royal Ptolomy,
Nor with Albumasar,
To treat of any star
Fixed or else mobile.
His Latin tongue doth hobble,
He doth but cloute and cobble
In Tully's faculty
Called humanity.
Yet proudly he dare pretend   530
How no man can him amend!
But have ye not heard this,
How an one-eyed man is
Well-sighted when
He is among blind men?

Then, our process for to stable,
This man was full unable
To reach to such degree,
Had not our prince be
Royal Henry the eighth,   540
Take him in such conceit
That he set him on height,
In exemplifying
Great Alexander the king,
In writing as we find
Which, of his royal mind
And of his noble pleasure
Transcending out of measure,
Thought to do a thing
That pertaineth to a king,   550
To make up one of nought,
And made to him be brought
A wretched poor man
Which his living won

With planting of leeks
By the days and by the weeks.
And of this poor vassal
He made a king royal,
And gave him a realm to rule
That occupied a shovel,   560
A mattock and a spade,
Before that he was made
A king, as I have told,
And ruled as he would
Such is a king's power
To make within an hour,
And work such a miracle,
That shall be a spectacle
Of renoun and worldly fame.
In likewise now the same   570
Cardinal is promoted,
Yet with lewd conditions coated
As hereafter been noted:
    Presumption and vainglory,
Envy, wrath, and lechery,
Covetise and gluttony;
Slothfull to do good,
Now frantic, now stark wood!
    Should this man of such mode
Rule the sword of might?   580
How can he do right?
For he will as soon smite
His friend as his foe!
(A proverb long ago.)

Set up a wretch on high,
In a throne triumphantly,
Make him a great estate,
And he will play checkmate
With royal majesty
Count himself as good as he;   590
A prelate potential
To rule under Belial,
As fierce and as cruel

As the fiend of hell! [. . .]
   No man dare come to the speech
Of this gentle Jack Breche,
Of what estate he be
Of spiritual dignity;
Nor duke of high degree,
Nor marquis, earl nor lord;   620
Which shrewdly doth accord!
   Thus he, born so base,
All noble men should outface,
His countenance like a kaiser.
'My lord is not at leisure.
Sir, ye must tarry a stound,
Till better leisure be found;
And sir, ye must dance attendance,
And take patient sufferance,
For my lord's grace   630
Hath now no time nor space
To speak with you as yet.'
   And thus they shall sit –
Choose them sit or flit,
Stand, walk, or ride –
And his leisure abide,
Perchance half a year;
And yet never thee near!

   This dangerous dowzypeer
Like a king's peer!   640
And within this sixteen years
He would have been right fain
To have been a chaplain,
And have taken right great pain
With a poor knight,
Whatsoever he hight!
The chief of his own counsel,
They cannot well tell
When they with him should mell,
He is so fierce and fell.   650
He rails and he rates,
He calleth them doddypates;

He grins and he gapes
As it were Jackanapes!
Such a mad Bedlam
For to rule this realm,
It is a wondrous case:
That the king's grace
Is toward him so minded,
And so far blinded,   660
That he cannot perceive
How he doth him deceive.
I doubt, lest by sorcery
Or such other loselry
As witchcraft or charming;
For he is the king's darling
And his sweet heart root,
And is governed by this mad coot. [. . .]

   Some men might ask a question,
By whose suggestion
I took on hand this work,
Thus boldly for to bark?
And men list to hark,
And my words mark,
I will answer like a clerk:
For truly and unfeigned,
I am forcibly constrained   1210
At Juvenal's request
To write of this glorious guest,
Of this vainglorious beast,
His fame to be increased
At every solemn feast,
Quia difficile est
Satiram non scribere. [. . .]

Notes

Womanhood, Wanton Ye Want (original: 'Womanhod, Wanton, Ye Want')

4 *recheles* heedless

13 *pohen* pea-hen

19 *shail* stumble

20 *piggesny* 'Pig's-eye': a flower and term of endearment

29 *farly* strange; dangerous

30 *wones* lives

Lullay, Lullay, Like a Child (original: 'Lullay, Lullay, Lyke a Chylde', from *Dyvers Balettys and Dyties Solacyous*)

8 *ba, ba . . .* baby-talk for 'kiss'

13 *prey* spoils, treasure

15 *rowth* rough

18 *halsed* embraced

20 *rowteth* snores

24 *blowboll* drunkard

28 *I wis . . .* 'I know, pole-axeman (or ale-pole haunter?), she pulled the wool over your eyes'

The Ancient Acquaintance (original: 'The Auncient Acquaintance', loc. cit.)

11 *Menolope* a queen of the Amazons

17, 18 *'Gup', 'Jaist ye', etc.* terms used to encourage horses

23 *kalkins . . .* she kicks with her horseshoes and kills with the nails

Ware the Lizard (original: 'Ware the Lesard', loc. cit.)

3 *rede* warn

5 *fell* skin

Mannerly Margery Milk and Ale (original: 'Manerly Margery Mylk and Ale', loc. cit.)

1 *beshrewe* curse

3 *popagay* parrot (proverbially proud)

5 *Tully valy*   worthless/nonsense (equivalent of 'pish')

6 *Christian Cloute*, etc.   dismissive (rural) nicknames (note Skelton's own later use of 'Colin Cloute' as a rustic persona)

8 *pode*   toad (as term of endearment)

16 *frumple*   wrinkle

To Mistress Margaret Hussey (original: 'To Mastres Margarete Hussey', from *The Garlande of Laurell*)

Margaret is probably the wife of John Hussey, one of the circle of the Howard family, at whose castle at Sheriff Hutton, Yorkshire, Skelton wrote *The Garland of Laurel* in the 1490s.

22 *Isaphill*   Hypsipyle, daughter of King Thoas of Lemnos, lover of Jason

23 *Colyaunder*   Coriander

25 *Cassaunder*   Cassandra, prophetess and princess of Troy

To Mistress Gertrude Statham (original: 'To Mastres Geretrude Statham', loc. cit.)

Gertrude is probably the wife of Roger Statham, another of the Howard circle. The text implies a more intimate relationship between poet and subject than in the previous lyric.

11 *Pasiphe*   Pasiphae, wife of King Minos of Crete, after sexual intercourse with a bull, she gave birth to the Minotaur. The allusion seems pointed

Against a Comely Coystrowne (original: 'Agaynste a Comely Coystrowne')

coystrowne   kitchen boy

countered   sang (the object of the invective is a rival musician)

6 *prendergest*   proud person

8 *bayard's bun*   horse loaf

11 *A maunchet . . .*   a fine white loaf for [a] black horse (i.e. pearls before swine)

15 *'With, Hey . . .'*   popular song refrains

18 *Martin Swart*   a German mercenary leader who aided the pretender Lambert Simnal against Henry VII

19 *Perkin*   possibly an allusion to another pretender, Perkin Warbeck

23 *solfeth, treble*   musical terms

25, 29 *pirdewy, Roty bully joyse*   other popular songs

34 *tavels*   cloth-making devices

43 *jet* flaunt himself
54 *prick song* the descant on a plain song
54 *plain* (song) unaccompanied Church singing
57 *Custodi nos* 'Preserve us': the opening line of a religious verse
59 *Sospitati* . . . 'He gave succour to the sick': a piece of sung devotional prose
69 *Written* . . . a deliberately nonsensical location and date (the Kalends is 1 May)

Philip Sparrow (edited version of the original: *Phyllyp Sparowe*)
The poem begins as a mock elegy on the death of a pet bird belonging to a young nun, Jane Scrope, of Carrow Abbey near Norwich. It intersperses Jane's lament for her bird with Latin passages from the Mass for the Dead.
1 *Pla ce bo* . . . the opening line of the Vespers for the Dead, taken from Psalm 114 (Vulgate)
9 *Nuns Black* Carrow was a Benedictine house
12 *bead-rolls* the list of the dead for whom prayers and masses were sung
16 *mead* reward
64 *Heu, heu* . . . 'Woe, woe is me!' (Psalm 119)
66 *Ad Dominum* . . . 'In my tribulation I cried to the Lord' (Psalm 119)
69 *marees* marsh/mire
70 *Acheronte* Acheron, one of the rivers of Hades
74, 78 *Alecto* and *Megera* the Furies Alecto and Megaera
83 *Proserpina* Queen of Hades
97 *Levavi* . . . 'I will lift up my eyes to the hills' (Psalm 120)
98 *Zenophontes* the Greek philosopher Xenophon
137 *gressop* grasshopper
143 *Si in i qui* . . . 'If thou markest iniquities' (Psalm 129)
145 *De pro* . . . 'Out of the depths I cried [unto the Lord]' (Psalm 129)
147 *dome* judgement
148 *Sulpicia* perhaps the poetess praised by Martial in his *Epigrams*
171 *perde* truly
183 *O pe ra* . . . 'The works . . .' (Psalm 137: 'Oh Lord, do not forsake the works of your own hands')
185 *Confitebor* . . . 'I will praise thee, Lord, with my whole heart' (Psalm 137)
191 *Attalus* King of Pergamum, a notable patron of the visual arts
194 *Cadmus* son of King Agenor of Tyre who searched for his sister Europa who had been abducted by Zeus
239 *A porta* . . . 'From the gates of Hell' (Matthew 16)

243 *Au di vi . . .* 'I heard a voice [from Heaven say unto me, write: 'blessed are the dead'], (Relevation 14)

244 *Japhet,* etc. the sons of Noah

247 *Armony* Armenia, the resting place of Noah's Ark

253 *Deucalion* classical analogue to Noah (see Ovid, *Metamorphoses*)

290 *Libany* Libya

296 *Melanchates* one of Acteon's hounds, traditionally the first to turn on his master once he had been transformed by Diana into a stag

309 *Arcady* Arcadia, Greece

311 *Lycaon* King of Arcadia, transformed into a wolf for sacrificing human flesh to Jupiter

318 *Occyan* the sea thought in medieval times to surround the lands of the earth

319 *Orchady* the Orkneys

362 *musse* mouth (beak)

379–81 *Kyrie . . .* 'Lord, have mercy/Christ, have mercy', etc.

386 *Lauda . . .* 'Praise the Lord, O my soul' (Psalm 145)

407 *spink* chaffinch

408 *shoveller* spoonbill

409 *doterell* a kind of plover

412 *fieldfare* a kind of thrush

412 *snite* snipe

424 *mavis* song-thrush

432 *bittern* bittern, the 'bump' being its characteristic booming call

434 *Menander* the Greek river Maeander

447 *gaggling gaunt* gannet

449 *route and cough* the knot and the ruff

452 *divendop* dabchick

468 *coe* jackdaw

478 *The ostrich* the ostrich was thought to be able to consume iron in its hot stomach

487 *To solfe . . .* to sing above the highest note: to overreach

488 *Ga, lorell . . .* 'stick to [lower notes such as] "fa", fool'

489 *Ne quando . . .* 'lest by singing badly'

524 *reflary* perfume

552 *sedean* sub-dean

565 *lanners and marlions* small hawks

567 *muskett* male sparrow-hawk

575 *Requiem . . .*   'grant them eternal rest, O Lord' (from the Vespers for the dead)

577 *A por ta . . .*   'from the gates of Hell'

579 *Credo . . .*   'I hope to see the goodness of the Lord' (Psalm 26)

581 *Domine . . .*   'Lord, hear my prayer' (Psalm 101)

583 *Do mi nus . . .*   'The Lord be with you'

585 *Oremus* 'Let us pray'

586 *Deus, cui . . .*   'Lord, whose nature is always to have mercy . . .'

616 *Palamon and Arcet*   Chaucer's *Knight's Tale*

629 *Gawain and Sir Guy*   Sir Gawain and Guy of Warwick, heroes of many medieval romances

649 *Sir Lybius*   Lybeaus Desconus, of the Romance of 'The Fair Unknown'

651 Quater Fylz Amund   *The Four Sons of Amun*, a version of which was to be printed by Caxton

656 *Bayard*   the horse of the four sons of Amun

664 *Paris and Vienne*   another romance later printed by Caxton

686 *ouche*   broach

734 *Marcus Marcellus*   Marcus Claudius Marcellus, victor at Syracuse in the second Punic War, killed by Hannibal

736 *Anteocus*   Antiochus III of Syria, who gave Hannibal asylum in 195 BC

737 *Josephus*   historian of the first century AD, author of the *Jewish Antiquities*

739 *Mardocheus*, etc.   the story is taken from the Book of Esther

742 *teen* anger

746 *Evander*   son of Hermes and Themis referred to in the *Aeneid*

747 *Porcena*   Lars Porsena, King of Clusium and ally of the exiled Tarquin's against Rome

752 *bougets and males*   wallets and purses

759 *Alchaeus or Sappho*   poets of Lesbos

779 *frowards*   difficulties (specifically here difficult words)

784 *Gower*   John Gower, poet and contemporary of Chaucer

804 *John Lydgate*   poet of the fifteenth century, author of *The Fall of Princes*

826 *Flos volucrum*, etc.   'Fair Flower of a bird, farewell. Philip, beneath that marble now you lie, you who were dear to me. Ever in the brighter sky will be shining stars, and you will ever be impressed in my heart.'

845 *Beati . . .*   'Blessed are the undefiled in the way' (Psalm 118), 'O glorious woman!'

860 *Arethusa*   the nymph evoked as a muse by Virgil in *Eclogue* X

875 *Tagus*   the Iberian river believed to contain golden sand

1018 *Lucres*   Lucrece, raped by Tarquin

1019 *Polexene*   Polyxena, daughter of Priam, desired by Achilles

1020 *Caliope*   Calliope, muse of epic poetry

1021 *Penelope*   wife of Odysseus, courted by many suitors in his absence

1029 *Memor . . .*   'Remember thy word unto thy servant. I am thy servant' (Psalm 118)

1034 *lere*   face

1061 *Bonitatem . . .*   'Thou hast dealt bountifully with thy servant, Lord' (Psalm 118)

1062 *Et ex . . .*   'And from the heart sound praises'

1090 *Defecit . . .*   'My soul fainteth after thy salvation' (Psalm 118); 'What seeketh thou for thy son, sweetest mother?'

1114 *Quomodo . . .*   'O, how I love thy law, O Lady!' (after Psalm 118); 'Old things are passed away, all things are new' (after Corinthians 5)

1124 *Unneth*   scarcely

1143 *Iniquos . . .*   'I hate vain thoughts. Let not the proud oppress me' (Psalm 118)

1152 *Egeria*   the wife of Numa, who wept so greatly on his death that she was transformed by Diana into a fountain

1157 *wood*   mad

1168 *Mirabilia . . .*   'Wonderful are thy testimonies' (Psalm 118); 'as plants grown up in their youth' (Psalm 143)

1192 *Clamavi . . .*   'I have cried with my whole heart, hear me!' (after Psalm 118)

1215 *Principes . . .*   'Princes have persecuted me without cause' (Psalm 118); 'All things considered, this girl is the sweetest of heavenly delights'

1238 *Requiem . . .*   'Give them eternal rest, O Lord'

1241 *Tibi . . .*   O Lord, thou hast searched me' (Psalm 138)

1242 *Saint James*   the shrine of St James at Compostella

Elynour Rummyng (edited version of the original: *Elynour Rummynge*) There was an ale-house-keeper called 'Alianora Romyng', who sold beer in Leatherhead in the 1520s.

1 *I chill*   I[ich] [w]ill

6 *grill*   fierce

12 *lere*   skin

17 *bowsy*   drink-sodden

25 *glare*   slimy

28 *camously*   snub-nosed
34 *gowndy*   gum-filled
45 *huckels*   hips
52 *jolly fet*   jollivet (pretty young girl)
53 *flocket*   sleeved cloak
54 *rocket*   smock
55 *cocket*   coquetry
61 *sere*   dried, withered
68 *gites*   clothes
75, 76 *whim-wham, trim-tram*   worthless ornaments
94 *wonning*   dwelling
99 *tunnish gib*   barrel-cat (drunkard)
102 *noppy ale*   sweet, frothy ale brewed from malted barley
105 *swinkers*   workers
142 *skewed*   mottled
148 *unlust*   unsavoury
150 *cawry-mawry*   [like] coarse cloth
151 *teggs*   yearling sheep
178 *frigs*   scratches
185–6 *ill preving, evil cheving*   a bad fate
218 *blee*   colour/complexion
223 *whiting, etc.*   diminutive terms of endearment
229 *fonny*   randy
254 *athrust*   thirsty
258 *slaty or slidder*   miry or slippery
269 *birl*   pour out
292 *tirly-tirlowe*   a song or dance tune
295 *hekell*   flax-comb
296 *rock*   distaff
298 *wharrow*   part of a spinning wheel
299 *ribskin*   leather work-apron
314 *chaffer*   goods
332 *go bet*   hurry
333 *met*   measure
334 *it was dear*   based on the proverb 'far-fetched goods cost dearest'
343 *fiest*   a fart
347 *calletts*   whores
358 *There hath been great war . . .*   nonsensical 'news'
365 *the pose*   a head-cold
553 *Wheywormed*   pimple-covered

561 *crop*   gullet

582 *pryckemedenty*   'prick-me-dainty': a prim woman

587 *lege de moy*   a kind of dance

589 *peevish-nice*   querulous

Against Garnesche (from *Poems Agenyst Garnesche*)

Garnesche   Sir Christopher Garnesche, Gentleman Usher to Henry VIII. From the texts of the full series of poems, it seems that the original altercation which prompted the flytyng (a formal exchange of poetic insults) began when Garnesche called Skelton 'knave' in the king's presence, a slight to which the poet demanded the right to respond.

3 *scribe*   by this stage in the flytyng, Garnesche was evidently employing a ghost-writer for his side of the exchanges

14 *lorell*   a rogue or knave

30 *fonne*   fool

33 *my lady Brews*   Lady Elizabeth Brews of Hasketon Hall, Suffolk

38 *hafting, polling*   deceit and stealing

40 *Guisnes*   Garnesche served there during Henry VIII's 1513 French campaign, but as Sergeant of the King's Tents rather than one of the King's Spears. Skelton perhaps refers to earlier military service there

46 *dud frese*   ragged, coarse woollen cloth

55 *. . . mistress Andelby*   these lines are damaged in the original text

62 *bassed*   kissed

72 *pikes, twibill*   pick-axe, small-bill or axe

90 *your scribe's noll*   'your scribe's head'

94 *dawpate*   idiot

101 *Bayard*   proverbially a blind horse

109 *Jack Raker*   scavenger: a favourite Skeltonic term of abuse

110 *craker*   boaster

129 *geson*   scanty

139 *shall cut both white and green*   Garnesche has evidently threatened to cut the white and green Tudor livery which Skelton wore

143 *puauntly*   stinkingly

155 *cast your craws*   vomit

157 *prick*   pitch

159 *serpentins*   a type of cannon

168 *gorgon glaimy*   slimy Gorgon

170 *murrion, mawment*   Moor, Mohammed

178 *pelfry . . .*   rubbish thou hast collected

179 *over-watched*   overreached

181 *meetly matched*   appropriately treated
182 *bedawed*   made into a fool
185 *Stokes*   the identity of 'Stokes', Garnesche's debtor, remains a
mystery
204 *Jake a Thrum*   an illiterate drunkard

Speak, Parrot (edited version of original: *Speke, Parott*)
10 *tote*   peep
28 *Quis . . .*   'Who taught the Parrot to say "hello"?'
29 *Dowche*   sweet
31 *Parlez bien . . .*   'Speak well, Parrot, or speak nothing'
37 *peerless pomegranate*   the pomegranate was one of Katherine of
Aragon's emblems
38 *saves . . .*   'can speak Castilian'
39 *fidasso . . .*   'have faith in yourself'
40 *Vis consilii,* etc.   'Strength without wisdom, as Horace teaches, falls by
its own weight'
42 *Soventez . . .*   'Many times, Parrot, in memory'
46 *pandes mory*   'grow mad'
47 *Phronesis*   understanding
49 *Salve . . .*   'On holiday it is best to have everything'
50 *Moderata . . .*   'Moderation delights: but everything is too much'
52 *Myden . . .*   'nothing in excess'
55 *Hec res . . .*   'This hits the nail on the head . . . by my faith'
56 *Tycez-vous . . .*   'Be quiet, Parrot, keep still'
59 *Vitulus*   the [golden] calf
60 *Melchisedeck*   Melchizedek, King of Salem, seems to stand here for
Henry VIII, while Moloch, bull-god of the Midianites, suggests Wolsey,
who is said to revel in the freedom which the king allows him
62 *cum sensu . . .*   'with a mature perception . . . Not too sane, and not too
mad'
64 *Aram . . .*   a series of biblical allusions generally suggestive of a realm
in crisis
68 *ebrius*   drunk
69 *lyver god . . .*   'Hush, dear God of Heaven, I say' (Dutch)
71 *Over in a whinnymeg*   'Over in an instant': the opening of a popular
ballad
72 *Hop Lobin*   a dismissive name suggesting the Scots, 'of Lothian'
73 *gibbet of Baldock*   Jack-o-Legs, a medieval outlaw, was hanged in
Baldock, Hertfordshire

78 *Ic Dien*   'I serve', the motto of Henry VIII as Prince of Wales, whose emblem was the ostrich feather

79 *Beme*   Bohemia

85 *Morrish*   slurred (mock-Irish) pronunciation of 'Morris'

86 *fate*   water (mock-Irish)

88 *moveatur . . .*   let the world go

89 *Sir Wrig-wrag,* etc.   mock knights

91 *Pawbe . . .*   'Everyone in his manner' (Welsh proverb)

93 *Aristippus*   a hedonistic Greek philosopher

95 *unde . . .*   'Whence I produce dilemmas taught in the sacred school of poets'

111 *Esebon*   the heathen city of Sihon, King of the Amorites, enemies of Israel

113 *Ulula*   weep

113 *Jeremy*   Jeremiah

114 *Rachel . . .*   Rachel (a type of the Church) looks ruefully

115 *Madionita . . .*   again the poet produces a vision of a land in chaos and despair through biblical allusion

121 *Seon . . .*   Sihon, of the 'Amorites', and Og, King of Bashan, retain 'the scullion of the Canaanites'. Again the reference for the 'fat' Og would seem to be Wolsey.

124 *assilum . . .*   'And sanctuary, once the refuge of the unhappy, is not sacred, but is to become secular.' Wolsey began to attack the rights of sanctuary held by ecclesiastical institutions, chiefly those of Westminster Abbey (within whose precincts Skelton lived) in these years.

127 *Weston next Barnet*   Bromhall Abbey, near Whetstone, was dissolved by Wolsey in 1521. It had a water-mill attached to its estate.

129 *chaffer far-fet*   goods far-fetched (proverbially expensive)

133 *Quod . . .*   'But Judas Escariot is a mighty lord' (again the allusion, here and above, would seem to be to Wolsey)

140a *Monon . . .*   'only the beautiful is good': or 'only the good is beautiful'; here Parrot gives an example of the perils of unsure translation

148 *phrisesomorum*   part of a syllogism. Parrot begins to attack the allegedly unscholarly practices of the Humanists who were introducing the study of Greek into the schools

149 *Formaliter . . .*   'Formally, and in Greek, with the middle term (of a syllogism)'

150 *Argolicorum*   'of the Greeks'

151 *phormio*   either a verbose fool, or a straw-mat

152 *Capricornio*   'in the dark'

155 *secundum . . .* the sense seems to be '[they argue] that what is true sometimes is true always'

156 *pro Areopagita* as one of the senators or judges

158 *ita* and *non* 'thus' and 'not' (quibbling distinctions)

160 *Sophia* wisdom

163 *Greci fari* 'to speak Greek'

166 *Trivials*, etc. The Trivium and Quadrivium, the academic syllabus

169 *Albertus* Albertus Magnus, mistakenly thought to be the author of two works, *liber Modorum Significandi* and *Questiones de Modis Significandi*

170 *Donatus* author of the *Ars Grammatica*, the standard school grammar textbook

171 *Prisian*, etc. other grammatical texts and exercises now disregarded by the reformers.

179 *'Aveto'* 'Good-morning' (Greek)

183 *cum gariopholo* [nutmeg] with cloves, taken for wind, and to clear the brain

185 *pleris . . .* an electuary with musk

191 *quasi . . .* 'Almost transparent, or like a mirror in a riddle'

196 *confuse tantum* 'so much confusion'

198 *confuse . . .* ordered confusion

203 *pavis* shield

209 *Melpomene* the tragic Muse

229 *Psitacius . . .* 'Parrot, behold, I sing: I know my songs are not worthy of Phoebus, yet my poem is full of God'

231 *secondum . . .* 'Next to the famous Skelton, counted in the book of the Muses'

232a *Itaque . . .* 'Wherefore, comfort one another with these words' (I Thessalonians 4)

232c *Galathea* the lover of Pamphilus in a popular poem

235 *My proper Besse* a popular song

278 *quire* book

279 *Jerobesethe* Jerubbesheth, Gideon (a figure for Wolsey here)

280 *cliffs of Scaloppe*, etc. allusions to locations in and around Calais

308 *grandepose* grampus

309 *the great seal* a punning allusion to the Great Seal which Wolsey carried as Chancellor and had taken to Calais with him, causing administrative paralysis at home in its absence

322b *Psitace . . .* 'Parrot, go quickly to turn back the arrows of fools. Shit! Pure slanders!'

326 *Sir Sydrake* another mocking epithet for Wolsey

339 *Non sine . . .* 'Not without a grimace behind his back'

345 *Monasticon . . .* 'Go quickly Parrot, and so refute all malicious tongues'

347 *Altior . . .* 'Higher, alas, than the cedar, more cruel, alas, than the leopard! The bull-calf of the ox [i.e. Wolsey] becomes the lord of Priam [i.e. Henry]'

349 *Non annis . . .* 'Granted that it is not because of your age, but because of your rank that you [Henry] are called Priam . . . so long as you cherish the calf, King of Britain, you are ruled: King, you are ruled, you do not yourself rule. Illustrious king, be wise, subdue the calf, in case he becomes too foolish'

359 *supply* supplicate

366 *jacounce* jacinth

369 *remorders* critics

371 *I, volitans . . .* 'Go, flying Parrot, curb your wit, scarcely will they understand who read your writings'

373 *Psitacus . . .* the sense is unclear, but the passage seems to compare the fame of Parrot with that of Persius

376 *O unice . . .* 'O only beloved, the entire jewel of my prayers, a precious stone is your covering'

377 *Sicut Aron . . .* 'Like Aaron and the people, so the ox-calf, so the ox-calf, etc.'

382a *Le Popagay . . .* 'The Parrot begins to complain'

387 *reckless* pointlessly

399 *Jupiter . . .* 'As Jupiter is worshipped in bright Olympus, he [Henry VIII] is worshipped here as a God. Incense is given to Jupiter, sitting on his golden throne, with Jupiter he [Henry] takes incense. Jupiter, ruler of the stars and lord of the poles, rules the English kingdom'

402 *mawmett* 'mohammed' (generally a demon)

412, 413 *Cleros, passe-a-Pase* punning references to Thomas Clark and Richard Pace, two English diplomats currently engaged on further English (Skelton would claim Wolsey's) foreign policy on the Continent

414 *Over Scarpery . . .* into Italy 'with evil hail'

415 *pendugims* penguins (here black coated clerics)

424 *nebbis* nose

426 *couch-quail* a children's game

433 *Skyre-galiard*, etc. lecher, whoremonger, big-talker

437 *ex qua . . .* a passage of largely untranslatable Latin, beginning 'from which power, from my verse . . .'

479 *papers wearing* a reference to the practice of making convicted felons wear publicly 'papers' describing the nature of their crimes

505 *right of a ram's horn* an oxymoron, a ram's horn being bent, and so not 'right'

517 *Pole-axes and pillers* references to Wolsey's ceremonial trappings. When processing to and from the courts, the Cardinal was attended by liveried retainers carrying gilt pole-axes and pillars

579 *Crescet . . .* 'This Parrot will grow greatly in my lifetime, Thus the glorious fame of me, Skelton will be celebrated'

Colin Cloute (edited version of original: *Colyn Cloute*)

Quis consurget . . . 'Who will rise up with me against evil doers? Or who will stand up with me against the workers of iniquity?' (Psalm 93 Vulgate) 'No one, Lord!'

17 *wotteth* knows

49 *Colin Cloute* from Latin 'Colonus': farmer, and 'cloute': rags, thus a poor ragged rustic

89 *the forked cap* a bishop's mitre, i.e. promotion

106 *ire and venire* coming and going

107 *solfa 'so . . .* musical notes

108 *praemunire* the law prohibiting foreign, chiefly papal, interference in strictly English jurisdictions

298 *Simoniac* a practitioner of simony, the buying and selling of clerical office

299 *Hermoniac* probably an Armenian: a priest of doubtful orthodoxy

305 *anchor* an anchorite

312 *paul* a fine cloth

316 *rotchettes* coats of fine Rennes linen worn by wealthy priests

324 *Jack of the Noke* the common man

331 *fairly* (a) wonder

347 *aquilonis . . .* princes of the north: Wolsey, as Archbishop of York, like Satan had his throne in the North

352 *prests* forced loans, a reference to the loans imposed upon London by Wolsey in 1522

365 *culerage* a pain (in the arse)

369 *Tenure . . .* tenure through foolishness, not service

372 *Littleton's Tenures* Sir Thomas Littleton's *Tenures* was the standard law book of the period

378 *In secula* to secular lives

380 *vagabundare . . .* 'wander like vagabonds through the market place,

and take a fee, against the rules of their order, whether [that] of the Austin Canons or the Benedictines or the Cistercians or the friars of the Holy Cross'

391 *sely* pious, innocent

399, 400 *fuck sails, ventales* foresails, part of a head-dress

401 *shales* stumbles

403 *lay fee people* the laity

417 *mell* meddle

418 *titivelles* gossips. Titivillus was the devil supposed to collect idle words spoken in church

444 *in deliciis . . .* 'in luxury, in glory and riches, in grand honour, in pomp and magnificence, with amazing wealth, living without chastity'

458 *hippocras* spiced wine

461 *per assimile* in like manner

471 *Ariete* Aries

705 *conquinate* pollute

720 *res certa* a certain thing

932 *predial lands* lands attached to a farm

953 *a* lege de moy a dance: these lines describe tapestries on classical subjects in Wolsey's palace at Hampton Court

1000 *Cum regibus . . .* 'to be friendly with kings, and to rule over everyone, is to overreach (or overburden) oneself'

Why Come Ye Not to Court? (extracts from original: *Why Come Ye Nat to Courte?*)

29 *Hec vates . . .* '[says] the famous poet whom a thousand quote'

35 *bass* kiss

53 *boskage* the woods

68 *'Dicken, thou Crow'* a popular song refrain

77 *countering at Cales* (Calais) the Calais conference of 1521

78 *males* wallets

95, 96 *favell, javell, etc.* flattery, knave, a series of vice-like figures

117 *cammock* branch

120 *the hare, etc.* allusions to the names or heraldic devices of magnates such as the Duke of Buckingham ('the buck') allegedly destroyed by Wolsey

126 *'ge heme'* (mock-scots) 'Go home!'

128 *tot quot* a dispensation

131 *lisle-wulsey* coarse woollen cloth (an obvious pun on 'Wolsey')

132 *Opus male . . .* 'a bitter-sweet work'

153 *Earl of Surrey* Thomas Howard, son of the victor of Flodden, whose campaigns in France Skelton contrasts with Wolsey's allegedly pacifist foreign policy

170 *scutus* scuts: French coins

188 *Chamber of Stars* the court of Star Chamber, over which Wolsey presided as Lord Chancellor

206 *Philargaria* avarice

211 *Dalyda* Delilah, more generally a whore

235 *kues* small, very low-value coins

236 *stews* the brothels of Southwark

272 *lord Dacres* Thomas Lord Dacre was the Warden of the northern Marches who agreed a truce with the Scots in 1522

288 *cockly fose* wrinkled leek

316 *sergeants of the Coif* lawyers

329 *huddy-peke* fool

386 *the hard arse* hard [i.e. close] by the arse, i.e. beheaded completely, to excess!

410 *York Place* York Place, Wolsey's official London residence as Archbishop

420 *law Tancred* Canon Law, after the thirteenth-century commentator Tancredus

425, 432, 433 *Fleet, Marshalsea, King's Bench* prisons in and around London

466 *Acidiam* spiritual sloth

475 *A cecitate . . .* 'From blindness of heart, deliver us, O Lord!'

478, 479 *Amaleck, Mamelek* an Old Testament figure (see Genesis 36); Mameluke, Turkish ruler

494 *butcher's stall* as Skelton repeatedly reminded him, Wolsey was a butcher's son

523 *Albumasar* Arab astrologer

528 *Tully* Marcus Tullius Cicero

544 *Alexander* the story refers to Abdalonimus, made King of Sidon by Alexander

592 *Belial* a devil

616 *Jack Breche* another contemptuous invention

639 *dowzypeer* (ironic) one of the *douze-pairs*, the noble companions of Charlemagne

652 *doddypates* blockheads

664 *loselry* knavish behaviour

1216 *Quia difficile* . . .   'because it is difficult not to write satire [nowa-
days]' (Juvenal)

Acknowledgements

I am grateful to my colleagues at the University of Leicester, especially Professor Gordon Campbell and Dr Elaine M. Treharne, for the help and advice offered during the editing of this collection, also to Margaret Wallace for her exemplary copy-editing of the draft text.